D1258325

PREPPING FOR LIFE

The Balanced Approach to Personal Security and Family Safety

GRANT CUNNINGHAM

Personal Security Institute LLC

FREE OFFER!

I've prepared a package of pre-made worksheets to help you put the lessons of Adaptive Personal Security to work in your life — and it's yours FREE!

Inside the Prepping For Life Worksheet Pack you'll find:

- The Preparedness Inventory worksheet, to help you catalog what you've already done and put it all into proper context to help you move forward
- The Threat Assessment worksheet, to help you figure out what you should really prepare for
- The Adaptive Personal Security Matrix, which is the key to planning and charting all your preparedness activities

All of them are in PDF format so you can print out as many as you need, plus I've included an Excel spreadsheet version of the Threat Assessment worksheet for instant Risk Index calculation!

Get your free Worksheet Pack at this link:

www.getgrant.us/prepping

CONTENTS

Part Four
RESPOND

ACKNOWLEDGMENTS

A book is rarely the work of just one person. Many people have contributed, directly or indirectly, to this project.

Thanks to Mitchell Lake, Associate Attorney at Rachel M. Baird & Associate in Harwinton, CT, for his insight in the legal discussions.

I appreciate the people who agreed to review and comment on the material here: Cecil Burch, Kim Campbell, Annette Chapman, Michael Dasargo, Thomas "TJ" Gauthier, Siddhartha Priest, and Phil Wong.

Special thanks to Joshua Gideon for his unwavering support and input.

As I've often said, behind every good writer is a great editor. I'm privileged to have one of the very best, Kathy Allard.

My wife of more than three decades, Chris, deserves the credit for inspiring the subjects about which I write, as well as keeping me on track when I wander.

Finally, thanks to YOU for supporting my work!

— *Grant Cunningham,* June 2017

INTRODUCTION

Some years ago, I picked up the nickname "the Tactical Hippie." It's true that my hair has gotten longer as I've gotten older, and I'm sure my hair has contributed to my image. At the same time, it must be said I do look at self-defense, home and family protection, disaster survival, and all the nasty stuff that can go wrong in life from a different viewpoint than most. I consider those things interrelated, part of a larger whole. I see them holistically, as being indivisible from my life and my happiness.

Being prepared is, to me, a peaceful activity.

Is self-defense peaceful?

Take self-defense, for instance: It's not that I reject violence. Instead I understand that violence, like any tool, has a proper place. Self-defense — which is simply one part of personal preparedness — isn't about going into the world with a conqueror's attitude. I don't study and teach these things so I may dominate others. I don't do it because I want to use violence. I do it in order that I don't need to.

The statement might seem paradoxical, but self-defense (and by extension all preparedness) is about living in peace, free from fear and coercion. It is the ultimate form of self-reliance: the ability to keep yourself and your loved ones from harm regardless of the source. That ability might include fighting back against criminal violence, but it might also include avoiding the conflict in the first place. The person who has the skills and knowledge to walk away from a conflict or save himself from it should he not be able to avoid it, knows a peace not available to those who don't have those abilities.

The same thing can be said about preparation for hurricanes, earthquakes, pandemics, auto accidents, or nuclear accidents. Knowing ahead of time that you'll be able to live to see your grandchildren, read more books, listen to great music, and have intimate dinners with your significant other is a tremendous mental liberator. Preparing for the worst should be a joyous thing!

Preparation isn't about fear, it's about peace

I'm obviously not suggesting you adopt a paranoid, fearful attitude while reading this book. Neither am I suggesting you become a Pollyanna. Living in a fantasy world only means you're constantly shutting out the reminders that reality isn't very far away. The fantasy world is really the most fearful world, because you know any little thing can cause it to fall apart. You might not want to admit it, but you know deep down it's true.

The real world, the one where you do need to prepare for the unexpected, is really the most free. Knowing that something could happen to you — be it a criminal attack or a natural disaster — is oddly and paradoxically freeing. By facing reality head-on and dealing with the possibilities by learning how to stay safe against them, you empower yourself. You make yourself braver, less fragile, and more resilient. You come away with the knowledge that you can shrug off the worst the world can throw at you, and survive to smell the flowers.

Yes, it's possible to allow paranoia to creep into a prepared lifestyle, and I can point you to lots of people who have. They live in fear because they don't have this perspective: You don't prepare because you fear death, you prepare because you love life. You prepare so you can wake up to another beautiful sunrise or the sound of children's laughter or birds singing, so evil doesn't ruin your life the way it has others'.

It's not all about guns

Peace is independent of the tools you have at hand. It's possible, and I've seen it many times, to be armed to the teeth and yet still be without peace. It's also possible to have few to no armaments on your person and be completely at ease. Your awareness of your world and your analysis of what you face and how you've prepared determine when you feel that peace.

Preparation means becoming resilient. Peace in resiliency means experiencing the serenity that is found in both the process and the result.

Lessons from a rainstorm

Have you ever put on a rainsuit and intentionally gone for a walk in a downpour? If you haven't, I highly recommend it; it's a remarkable feeling. The suit protects you from the cold water and you're free to walk around without a care, enjoying the unique sights and sounds of a city (or a forest or a beach) during a storm. While everyone around you is rushing for the nearest doorway, desperately trying to stay dry under an umbrella being blown about by the wind, you amble along without a care. It's like having a suit of armor protecting you from the slings and arrows of the raindrops.

Peace, in the sense I'm using the word, is just like that. Peace doesn't mean the absence of danger or risk, or even the ability to retaliate against them. Rather, peace comes from having balance. Balance happens when you know and understand the potential dangers in your environment, and at the same time know that your skills and preparations are sufficient to survive them. Without balance between your capabilities and the dangers you face, there is no peace, and balance only occurs when you're aware both of what you **need** to do and what you **can** do.

The rainsuit gives you balance — parity — against the rain. You know the suit is sufficient to keep you dry in the worst conditions, and the storm that ruins everyone else's day is only a slight inconvenience to you. You are resilient because you are prepared.

Your personal security, your preparedness, is the same thing on a larger scale. Think of it as the rainsuit for your entire life, giving you parity over the things that could dramatically alter your existence. But how do you get from where you are now to that point of happy resilience?

That's what this book is all about: showing you a systematic way to achieve balance in your training and preparations regardless of where you live, what you do, or where you go.

Your personal preparedness

Personal security is the ultimate reason for preparedness in all its forms. While the term "prepping" has picked up something of a bad connotation in recent years (thank you, reality television), the fact is if you do almost anything with your future in mind, you're a prepper! Preparedness is nothing more than making contingency plans for an unknown future. Self-protection, home defense, and family safety are all part of preparedness. If you hold a fire drill at home — and you should — you're prepping. You may not recognize it as such, but you most assuredly are!

This book isn't just about self-defense and family protection, though a large portion of it deals with those topics. The ideas and procedures we'll explore are equally applicable to all forms of preparedness. The framework I'll introduce later will help you prepare for a wide range of threats, from criminal to natural to accidental. Everything is focused on helping you survive a life-altering event with as little long-term disruption as possible.

In fact, it's easier to see where your self-defense plans fit into your life if you're able to step back and see them as part of the total fabric of your emergency preparations. Your first aid kits, fire extinguishers, and emergency generator all serve the same basic function as your concealed-carry firearm: They all address the same needs, which are preventing or minimizing the disruption of the life you're living.

Ultimately this book is about building your personal resiliency: your capacity to recover quickly from adversity. As you become more resilient, you'll hopefully teach your children how to do the same. Perhaps they'll teach their children, and so on. By taking little steps today, you can not only ensure the continuation of your own life, but build a legacy that will make your descendants safer and happier too!

How this book came about

I developed this approach to preparedness because of a personal need. In March 1993, my wife and I were jolted out of our beds by an earthquake. Here in the Pacific Northwest, earthquakes are not uncommon, but they tend to be very minor. In most cases, people don't even notice they've happened.

This one was different. It shook our house violently for about 30 or 45 seconds, knocking things off shelves and significantly moving our furnace and water heater — both gas-fired. Luckily no real damage was done, but others weren't so lucky. The quake significantly damaged many buildings, and an entire wing of our state capitol had to be closed for structural repairs.

Even so, this quake was mild compared to a future subduction zone event, which is almost an inevitability in our region. What would happen to us if the "big one" hit?

That morning, the reality of life in an earthquake zone was illustrated in dramatic fashion. I started wondering about our preparedness and how we could survive a wide range of threats on our lives. As I contemplated all the things we might need to do, I rapidly became overwhelmed. In our geographical area, we might need to deal with earthquakes, ice storms, wind storms, severe flooding, toxic spills, and much more. This didn't even take into account auto accidents or personal medical emergencies.

Around the same time, I'd started studying personal defense on a serious basis, learning about defensive shooting and how to deal with criminal attackers. This led to concerns about preventing crime at our home and dealing with attacks at work. This all quickly became overwhelming, and the now infamous "Y2K" fiasco only added to the things I had to be concerned about. What if the end-of-the-world nutcases were right?

All those things seemed independent of each other. They had no apparent relation. Sometimes they even seemed to compete for my attention, and I could see no way to reconcile them.

It wasn't until after the turn of the 21st century that I stumbled across the answer. I'd been involved with disaster response at our county Sheriff's office and was invited to do the coursework that would lead to a degree in emergency management. The great part, from my standpoint, was it wouldn't cost me a dime — the state was footing the tab. How could I say no?

What I learned from my studies was a new way of looking at preparedness. Instead of the haphazard and often unbalanced approaches of most preppers, I discovered how the professionals went about planning and preparing for a wide range of possible events. I took that knowledge and downsized it to fit the needs of a couple or a family rather than the needs of a city or state. The result is Adaptive Personal Security, a structured yet flexible approach to personal preparedness that makes it easy to understand what you need to do and why.

When I started to apply the principles you'll learn in this book, I could see how everything I was doing fit together into a cohesive whole. I could see where I was over-prepared, where I was under-prepared, and where I had wasteful duplication of effort and/or resources. I suddenly understood how defensive shooting and medical response are related and how I could make small changes to noticeably increase the range of circumstances I was prepared to face. I found myself in balance and at ease for the first time in years. The goal I'd wanted for my preparedness activities had finally been realized: internal peace.

Whether you're going all-in with disaster readiness or simply trying to keep bad people away from your family, the Adaptive Personal Security framework will help you do it more efficiently. Let's get started!

WHAT IS ADAPTIVE PERSONAL SECURITY?

In the past, books about self-defense, personal security, preparedness, and related topics all tended to focus on very discrete parts of the total safety picture. For instance, books on self-defense typically focused on what I call the Respond function: what you do when someone attacks you. Whether about martial arts or defensive shooting (and I've written my share of the latter), they're all concerned with what you do when the bad thing has already happened. They're really "self-rescue" books. To be fair, some of them go beyond mere response. But they very rarely, if ever, do much more than offer platitudes and safety tips without context.

Let's take the area of defensive shooting as an example. The existing books and classes almost always focus on pulling the trigger (or getting to the point when you can pull the trigger). Some include a perfunctory lecture on "mindset," and occasionally they talk about "situational awareness," but none tell you how to practice putting all those skills together. Shooting books tell you all about bullets and stances — but rarely give you any sort of structured practice instructions for your trip to the range.

It's the classic case of not being able to see the forest for the trees.

While you're spending your time and energy admiring the tree in front of you, one that's just as pretty is behind you — and to your side. You never see the others because you're fixated on the one that caught your attention. The net result is that you come out knowing a lot about one tree, but almost nothing about the forest in which it exists. Your personal safety has large and serious gaps.

Threats are more than just criminals

I'll bet when I say the word "threat," your mind immediately conjures up images of a bad guy in a hoodie robbing you at knifepoint. But that's a very narrow view of danger. Many things in this world can injure or kill you beyond the guy with the knife, and many more things can result in severe, disabling injuries. When you look beyond criminal attacks, you realize there is an almost endless variety of events that would cause significant disruption in your life. Natural disasters, pandemics, fires, even a car accident or the long-term loss of a job will all affect your life negatively and perhaps even change the entire course of your existence.

Doesn't it make sense to prepare for those, too?

That's why I wrote this book. It's my goal to give you the tools you need to see the whole forest of personal security and still be able to appreciate each tree in it. I hope that what follows leaves you better prepared, more confident, and truly secure in your existence.

Sounds like a tall order, doesn't it? But it's achievable if you approach your preparedness in a systematic way. To do that, you need the right framework.

The Adaptive Personal Security approach

In the following chapters, I show you how to set that framework up — a framework that serves several purposes:

- Gives you context for all those skills you've learned and all that gear you've acquired
- Helps you identify areas in which you're under-prepared
- Shows you where you're over-prepared
- Provides a guide for where you need to direct your preparations
- Allows you to integrate crime prevention with other preparedness activities
- Gives you a way to see interrelationships among all aspects of your personal safety
- Involves your family and loved ones in an overall safety and security plan

Eventually you'll realize that stocking up on non-perishable food, carrying a defensive weapon, and having a trauma kit in your briefcase and a flashlight in your pocket are all parts of a balanced whole: the protection of your life and the lives of your loved ones.

And most importantly, you'll have a way to get there from wherever you are now!

What does Adaptive Personal Security mean?

The term comes from the world of information security, where sensitive or valuable data is protected from all forms of loss. This may seem to be totally unrelated to securing your life and achieving the peace that comes from balance, but in reality it's not.

The "adaptive" part of the title is what's important. Adaptive security provides a framework that allows systems to identify threats and respond to them, even if the threat was unknown when the framework was devised. If you think about it, hackers and data thieves are constantly looking for new ways to access the data they want. Any security system based solely on past attacks would be useless every time a new type of attack was launched. And those new attacks happen daily, if not hourly.

An adaptive framework doesn't rely on specific solutions to specific problems. Instead, it's built to identify vulnerabilities and understand key functions so it can change and adapt as each new threat emerges. To use an analogy, instead of trying to figure out how to build a better mousetrap, it focuses on dealing with the mouse — which may include the mousetrap, but also lots of other things like not leaving the cheese out on the counter!

How can you use this adaptive approach in your own life?

The problem is that it's impossible to prepare for everything. Even preparing for a small subset of everything can be overwhelming! There are a lot of details, overlap, and conflicting choices. It's hard to see how everything interrelates and how preparing in one area can either hinder or help preparing in another.

This is where the Adaptive Personal Security system really shines. By breaking down your personal security into bite-size morsels, then addressing them in a systematic way, you'll be able to see the best way to use your limited preparation resources. Taking an adaptive approach to personal security means being able to respond to the greatest range of threats and making the best use of your resources in doing so.

You start with what you know, break down how to prepare for those things, and then see what commonalities they have. You can then structure your future preparations to cover as many different scenarios as possible. Instead of preparing for an earthquake, for instance, you think in terms of losing your home — which can happen from a number of other events as well. By preparing intelligently for one, you can prepare for them all.

That's the beauty of the adaptive approach to personal security. It helps you stay safe from the widest range of threats with the least amount of time, effort, money, and mental anguish.

The structure of Adaptive Personal Security

Adaptive Personal Security (APS) rests in three key structural areas: Deter, Detect, and Respond. Tying them all together and helping manage them is an administrative function we'll call Anticipate.

Deter: putting into place structures and procedures designed to keep dangers from turning into proximate threats. Basically, keeping the danger away from you through physical, psychological, and social engineering means.

Detect: learning how to spot emerging threats so you can avoid them — or at least be proactive about facing them. It's all about avoiding surprise and giving you time and space to mount a defense.

Respond: what you do in an active event to protect yourself and your loved ones, and what you do in the immediate aftermath to recover from the experience. If Deter and Detect fail, Respond is what you do when you're caught off-balance and forced to deal with the threat.

Anticipate: this is where everything starts and where a large portion of your energy and attention are placed. Anticipation is the basis for all of your security. It involves learning what threats you face, what approach is best to survive them, and making preparation and contingency plans. It's where you make decisions about what threats you most need to defend against and how you're going to do that. Anticipation is where you acquire the skills, equipment, and knowledge to implement and manage Deter, Detect, and Respond, and then practice implementing them in as realistic a manner as possible.

Putting it all together

We cover each of these components in depth, allowing you to see how each applies in various areas of your personal preparedness. It's important, though, that you understand each function as a component: a discrete but interrelated part of the whole, as opposed to a step in a linear activity. Adaptive Personal Security is not a flowchart! Instead, the components each contribute something specific to your security and work in tandem with the others to provide the overall protection you need.

HOW TO USE THIS BOOK

I hate to use militaristic terms, but this is a book about strategy — not tactics.

What follows is, by nature, very wide-ranging. When you consider your personal security as a cohesive and interrelated whole, you naturally need to consider many different things in Deter, Detect, and Respond. The purposes of this book are to help you see the whole picture and give you a way to work on all the pieces, not to tell you what those pieces should be.

As a result, I don't go into great detail about the specifics of any one part of your personal security. For instance, you won't find instructions on what guns to buy or how to use a tourniquet. Instead I help you figure out which of those skills you need to know and give you a game plan for learning and implementing them.

The Adaptive Personal Security approach is a flexible guide — a framework — that allows you to see where all your preparations fit in to your overall safety. Whether those preparations are classes you've taken, gear you've purchased, or skills you've learned, every one of them fits into the framework somewhere. If one doesn't, it's probably not an important part of your personal or family security.

For example, your assessment of your own life might indicate you'd benefit from a book on situational awareness or a class on defending your home with a firearm. Perhaps it would show you what you need is a hands-on workshop in dealing with severe trauma, or even how to escape from a chokehold. The Adaptive Personal Security framework lets you discover what you need and then helps you systematically invest the resources (time, energy, money, and interest) needed to add them to your preparedness arsenal.

In the section on surveillance systems, for instance, you'll find a brief overview of the benefits of modern connected video cameras. I don't supply configuration and installation instructions, nor do I explain in detail the many functions of those marvelous pieces of technology. I don't even make any specific hardware or software recommendations. If you decide you want to install such a system and that you want to do it yourself, you can find many resources by searching online.

To get started, you need to know where you stand at this moment in time. What is the balance in your preparedness bank account?

Exercise: Figure out where you stand

A Preparedness Inventory is a way for you to figure out what you need to do for your long-term security. Even if you do none of the other exercises in this book, it's important to do this one, because it shows you where you are now and where you may need to go.

1. Make a list of all your preparedness activities up to this point. "Activities" mean gear acquisitions, training, and skills.

2. Identify what threat (or threats) each activity addresses, and into which functional part(s) of the framework you believe each activity fits: Deter, Detect, or Respond.

3. For each, ask yourself if you've sufficiently addressed both the threat and the function. Mark it "finished" or "working on it" as appropriate.

4. Write down what additional things you think you need to do in order to be fully prepared in that specific area.

I encourage you not to skip this step or do it half-heartedly. You're unlikely to get the most out of Adaptive Personal Security without the insights it provides.

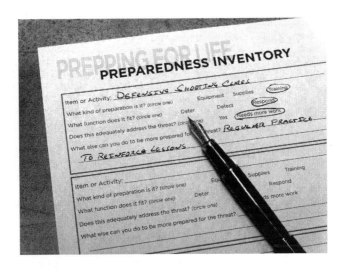

I've made a Preparedness Inventory form to help you with this step. It comes in the Prepping For Life Worksheet Pack, along with the Matrix and Threat Assessment forms you'll be introduced to later. You can get them all for free at this link:

www.getgrant.us/prepping

Preparedness budgeting

Why is it important to keep track of what you're doing and where it fits? Remember the goal I talked about at the beginning of the book: to be able to live a peaceful life. Keeping track of your preparations is how you know you've covered the most important bases and that you're spending your preparedness resources wisely.

Again, this is similar to budgeting. Not everyone has a strict budget that they follow to the penny, but those with good money management skills at least know where their money is going and what their check-book balance is. I'm certainly not suggesting you become an accountant with regard to your personal preparedness, but I am suggesting you have a clear picture of what you're doing and why. The best way to do so is to keep track of what you're doing — and why.

If you're the obsessive-compulsive type (as I tend to be), you can certainly indulge yourself inside of the APS structure! That's the beauty of it, and why the first word in the title is "adaptive": no matter how you want to approach your own preparedness, no matter what level of detail you like, the framework will make you better at using your resources and more secure in the results.

Pick your own approach

Once you know your current preparedness balance, you might decide to work through each function for a specific threat, making some progress in each before moving on to addressing a different danger. You could choose to work on just planning for all your identified threats first, then adding in the other functions on a rotating basis. It's possible to train and equip for Response above all else, because you feel it's the most important function. Or you could choose to do something entirely different.

All are valid, and I urge you to do what you believe is best for you.

How the functions fit together

Regardless of how you work through the functions, Anticipate, Deter, and Detect are perennial. You're always working on them or they're always working for you. You're either maintaining them or actively utilizing them. They're the things that actually keep you safe, in the sense that they're all about prevention. They're proactive.

The Respond function is a little different. In fact, it's not so much a component as it is a phase: you enter Respond when the threat presents itself. Respond encompasses those things you do when the threat you've prepared for is actually visited upon you. For instance, if one of the threats you've identified is a home invasion crime (which is something everyone should probably consider), Deter and Detect should always be operating even if you're not actively engaged in those functions at the moment. In other words, you've put them in place so you'll avoid the home invasion by making your house a less inviting target for home invaders.

Should the worst happen and those invaders do manage to kick in your door, the skills and resources you've prepared for the Respond function come into play. If the home invaders actually strike, the Deter and Detect security measures you put into place as part of the Anticipation process set you up for a successful Response. Working together, they decrease the likelihood you'll ever need a Response, and at the same time ensure it is timely and effective if needed.

They all matter, but you should aspire to so thoroughly implement Deter and Detect that Respond is never needed. This isn't any sort of guarantee, of course, because some things are simply too far out of your control. But striving for that condition is how you achieve the balance that brings you peace in your life. The Anticipation process helps you do that.

Don't panic!

Other than this exercise, very little in this book is written in stone. I don't say you must do every single step in the following chapters, or do them in some predefined and inviolate order. Instead, I encourage you to dive in where you feel you need to! The only important thing is to keep track of what you're doing, what threat it addresses, and into which function of the APS framework it fits.

While I believe using the framework to its fullest will help you live a much more relaxed life, the reality is that doing anything more than you're doing right now will be a benefit. You get to decide how far you want to go. No matter what your decision, Adaptive Personal Security will help you get there.

Part One

ANTICIPATE

This section of the book is simultaneously the most interesting and the most boring!

It's also the most important.

The Anticipation function of the Adaptive Personal Security framework is where most of your preparation actually happens. "Anticipate" means to be aware of what could happen in the future and to take action in order to be prepared. The Anticipation function is where you develop your expectation and prediction of what could interfere with your life. It's also where you put together your plans to be ready when anything happens.

Most preparation is anticipating

Anticipation is made up of your contingency planning, your preparations, and the exercise of your Responses to improve them over time. It's about researching, designing, testing, and refining.

For instance, if you take a defensive shooting class, it's part of Anticipation because it's the tool you'll use in the Respond function if you're attacked. If your Deterrence doesn't keep the criminal attacker away, you'll need to be able to defend yourself from him. But up to the point an attack happens, taking the class and practicing the skills you learn are part of Anticipation.

Selecting, buying, and installing an alarm system are part of Anticipation as well. When it's finally installed and working, it becomes part of your Detect function. Your security door? It's definitely a Deter function, but deciding which one to install and then actually installing it are a natural part of your planning in the Anticipate stage.

Everything that exists as part of your preparations starts in and comes from the Anticipate function. It's is where you monitor all the other functions of your preparedness framework — Deter, Detect, and Respond — decide which activities fit into each, and do the training and acquisitions to fill the gaps.

There's a lot going on in the Anticipate function, and while you may end up with numerous pieces involved, it comes down to just a few steps:

- Determine the dangers (threats) you face
- Figure out how you'll deal with them in each of the active functions: Deter, Detect, and Respond
- Acquire the skills and equipment you need (training and gear — or hardware and software, if you prefer those terms)
- Practice putting your skills and equipment to use
- Evaluate and learn from your mistakes

Eyes on the prize

Keep your focus on preventing — to the greatest degree possible — any given danger from affecting you. That's what safety is! Safety isn't about rescuing yourself. It's about not needing the rescue in the first place. It's better to keep the mugger from targeting you than it is to have to shoot him.

Keep the end in mind. The reason you prepare is to avoid disruption in your life. The best way to do so is to never be in a position where you come face to face with your threat.

EVERYTHING STARTS WITH A PLAN

I admit my reputation as the Tactical Hippie is somewhat at odds with the idea of planning. It may even seem at odds with the notions of peace and balance!

In fact I often think the same thing as I work on my preparedness plans, but the reality is, without some amount of organization, even the simplest goals can founder on the rocks of indecision. Only by having sufficient structure will most of us be able to spot what we need to focus on and recognize when we've reached a point of sufficiency.

Of course too much structure can be as bad as too little! Having too much system overhead, or tasks you must do or provide just to keep the structure operating isn't any good either. Excessive system overhead is why many people give up on time management systems, for instance.

In this book, I try to walk that fine line between too much and too little organization. My line may be different than yours, so feel free to adopt as much as you're comfortable with. If, over time, you find you want to take on more, that's terrific; just don't feel obligated to. Seek your own balance.

The value of planning

Many years ago, my wife and I decided we needed to do something about our home security. We were living in a suburban area with rapidly increasing property values. Of course, as the neighborhood became more exclusive, it also became more alluring to criminals.

Faced with the fear of the unknown criminal attack, we did what many people in our situation do: We bought a gun and went to the shooting range.

If you know me from my earlier works, you'll recognize me as being a "gun guy," but I wasn't way back then. I'd grown up with guns on the family farm and had been a hunter since childhood, but I knew very little about the defensive uses of a firearm. I became interested in defensive shooting as a result of my interest in the security of my home.

Shooting a gun at the range was a lot of fun, but the big problem was that the gun hadn't addressed our real concerns. As you may have heard me say, the lawfully possessed firearm is an efficient Response tool for a very small percentage of interpersonal conflicts. It doesn't keep anyone safe in the sense of preventing bad things from happening. It's a rescue tool, not a prevention strategy. My wife and I weren't substantially better off for having our gun, but we felt safer.

It wasn't until years later that the reality of the situation began to dawn on me: We needed more than the gun. But exactly what we needed wasn't clear, because the whole prospect of home security was so vast. Did we need an alarm, motion-sensing lights, a security door, surveillance cameras, motion detectors, a guard dog, steel bars on the windows, or something else entirely?

We had no way of mapping the forest, so we were left staring at individual trees. What we needed was something that could help us see the overall picture and figure out where each of those aforementioned security pieces fit. It would also help if we could figure out what we should do first. What we needed was a plan.

As our planning took shape, it became clear that our safety was a bigger project than we'd originally thought. We'd focused on bad guys getting into our house, but criminals weren't the only things in the world that could put us in the hospital (or the mortuary). As we expanded our thinking about safety, it became clear our existing plan wasn't sufficient to handle all the threats we actually faced. We had to shift from being intruder-centric to being preparedness-centric.

The seeds of Adaptive Personal Security had been planted.

What your plan does

Your plan is the most important part of your preparedness. It's where most of the work happens. Everything else, including your Responses in the face of danger, depend on how well you plan. The plan is the core of the framework, because it codifies how you'll equip, train, test, and optimize all your preparations. I cannot overstate its importance.

But first, you need to know what you're planning for.

Why plan? Why not just do everything?

You might be wondering why this framework is even necessary. Why can't you just prepare for everything? After all, you can't know what will happen in the future, so why go to all this trouble?

It's simple: you can't prepare for everything. It's not possible, and it's foolish to even try. You simply don't have the resources — time, energy, money, or interest — to prepare for everything that could possibly happen to you. But don't feel bad, because no one does!

In economics, there is a concept known as "opportunity cost": The loss of potential gain from other alternatives when one alternative is chosen. It is the basic relationship between scarcity and choice. Making a decision to spend your time, effort, interest, or money on one thing means you give up gain in some other area. Opportunity cost is real. Don't let yourself believe it's not. Doing one thing always means you give up something else to do it.

If you can't prepare for everything, you need to prepare for those dangers that are specific to your life and to a level that's appropriate for you. Everyone needs to seek their own balance — where they're prepared enough to feel peaceful — and to do that you need to identify the threats that are worth preparing for and let the rest of them go.

But how do you decide what's worth preparing for? We get into that discussion more deeply in the section on threat assessment, but first you need to come to grips with the reality that not everything is worth preparing for. Some dangers make sense to prepare for and some don't. How do you tell the difference?

The best way I've found is to understand the States of Expectation — Possible, Likely, and Plausible — and how they help you determine your own balance point.

Possibility

Many things in this world are ***possible***, in the sense that the laws of physics do not preclude them. But this doesn't mean all those things are equally likely to occur. Many, perhaps most, of the things that are possible are exceedingly unlikely to happen.

Possible events are all those things that could happen merely because the laws of physics allow them. Life has a huge range of possibilities, but not everything that is possible will actually happen. Think of it this way: Everything that could happen is possible, but not everything that's possible could really happen!

Likelihood

Likely events, on the other hand, are those that you can reasonably expect to happen. They have some mathematical certainty to them, largely because they happen just often enough that we can establish some level of probability as to their occurrence. In fact, ***probable*** is another way to express the concept of likelihood. Likely events are those which we can have some expectation of happening. Likely skills or tools are those for which there is some expectation of need.

Plausibility

Between possible and likely exists a third level of expectation: **plausible**. These are events that could happen because there is some historical basis for them happening. In other words, while they don't happen often enough to be certain or even mathematically likely, they've happened often enough that they could reasonably be believed to occur in your life. They may also be the logical expected result of some foreseeable if not common combination of events. These are those things you don't expect to happen, but aren't terribly surprised by when they do.

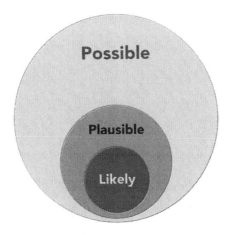

Why understanding expectation is important

Again, no one has an unlimited amount of time, energy, money, and interest to prepare for everything that is possible. Opportunity cost must be considered. Something has to give: If you train and equip for North Korean paratroopers taking over your local shopping mall, that's time/money/effort/interest you can't use to prepare for burglars. You need to prioritize what you do in order to establish a way of deciding what skills to learn and practice, what tools to procure, and what arrangements to make. Otherwise you might end up wasting your resources on things that don't impact your security. That's no way to achieve balance and peace!

It makes sense to first prepare for events that fall into the likely category. Once you've equipped yourself and developed the skills to deal with those, you can expand the application of your core skills to plausible events. If an event falls outside of the plausible category, it's merely a possibility and probably shouldn't merit much (if any) of your preparation resources.

Again, think of it like budgeting: You can't afford everything, so decide what's important to you and spend your money on those things first. It's the same idea. If you waste your resources or spend them unwisely, you'll be over-prepared in some areas and under-prepared in others. You can't reach your balance point.

Beyond events

I've framed this discussion so far in terms of events and incidents, of things that happen to you. Understanding the likelihood of any event helps you budget your preparation resources: time, money, energy, and interest.

Your expectation of using a particular skill or tool also falls into one of the states. For any given incident or event, there are skills you're likely to need, skills you might plausibly need, and skills that fall into the range of mere possibility. Training skills or acquiring tools that aren't of likely or even plausible need is a waste of your preparation resources, just as it is in preparing for specific kinds of events.

There is no substitute for thinking about these things, but haphazard or unorganized thinking does you no good. Many details, many nested states of expectation, can stall or derail your progress. By looking at your personal and family security preparations in a structured manner, you'll be able to see where you're over- and under-prepared and make the adjustments necessary to bring you back to balance.

That's the goal of Adaptive Personal Security: to give you a flexible structure so you know where it's best for you to spend your preparedness resources!

The "Worst-Case Scenario"

In this book, I talk about training and equipping yourself to survive the worst-case scenario. First I think it's important to explain the term. Most people get it wrong.

When I say "worst case," I don't mean the very worst event you can possibly imagine. Too many times, those sorts of doomsday scenarios are used to scare people into buying a particular point of view (or even a particular product). You can imagine all kinds of bad things that just aren't going to happen, and wasting your time worrying about them is counter-productive to living a peaceful life. Those worries lead to the constant fear we're preparing to avoid!

Instead, I mean the worst case of any particular type that you're likely to experience in your life. We're back to the discussion about states of expectation: The worst case I'm talking about is the one you can expect, based on your environment, lifestyle, and many other factors. Your worst-case scenario is going to be different than someone else's, because your life is different.

The worst-case scenario isn't a single event, either. For every threat you identify, there is a worst case. In our household, we prepare for earthquakes because they're common where I live. I've been through a couple of good ones, one of which resulted in widespread property damage (though, thankfully, no fatalities). The worst-case scenario for our earthquake preparations is the anticipated subduction zone earthquake that levels the West Coast. It will destroy homes, bridges, and possibly even dams, and bring massive tsunamis to take out what the earthquake left standing. Tens of thousands of people will likely die, and the toll could be higher depending on how powerful it turns out to be.

It's the worst likely case because science tells us it's almost inevitable (because it's happened many times over the history of the earth) and because it's historically overdue. It's almost a certainty to happen — but not necessarily in my lifetime, given the scale of geologic activity. It could happen while I'm writing this sentence (it clearly didn't), or it could happen 50 years from now. We know it's coming, we just don't yet have the means to predict exactly when. That's why, for where I live, it's the worst case.

Let's think about something a little more widespread: criminal attacks. Your worst-case scenario might be a home invasion with multiple attackers while you're asleep — catching you completely off guard and essentially at their mercy. Someone else might see the worst case a little differently. For each, though, the preparation goal is the same: being able to survive the most severe or potentially dangerous version of that particular threat that is likely to happen.

If what actually happens isn't as bad as the worst case, it's an easy-to-live-with bonus!

WHAT DANGERS DO YOU FACE?

Step One: Identifying threats

If you don't know what you're preparing for, it's difficult to do any preparation. Your first steps are figuring out which things can significantly affect your life, and then deciding which of those is worth preparing to face.

The pros refer to this as threat assessment: identifying the dangers you face and how important each is to your planning process.

The first step in threat assessment is to sit and think about yourself. Well, more precisely, think about:

- Your life, your activities, where you go and what you do
- Your home, where it's located and how it's laid out.
- Where you go on vacation, what hobbies you have, what you do for leisure and recreation
- The places outside of the home where you often spend time: work, house of worship, board meetings, sports activities
- Your physical condition
- How you get from place to place, and the routes you often

take. Does weather affect your travel? Do you cross any
bridges or go through congested urban areas?

Like I said, think about yourself. Write down all the activities in which
you regularly (or plan to) engage. How do you get there, and what do
you do when you arrive? If you're like most people, you'll end up with
several pages of notes reflecting your life and how you live it.

Once you've got those notes, do some consolidation. For instance,
getting your hair cut every month and going to the bank every week
are the same from a threat-assessment standpoint: You probably drive
there, spend some time standing or sitting while waiting for your
service to be performed, and then go home. Your risk of a carjacking,
being in the middle of a robbery, a traffic accident, or a fire are probably the same in both activities. Consolidate all the things with the
same (or approximately the same) risks together.

After consolidation, you'll probably find you face only a handful of
major dangers. Those are the ones you need to pay attention to.

It's useful to repeat this exercise for every member of your household.
Their activities may not be exactly like yours, and as a result their
threat assessment may be slightly different. If your goal is to make your
whole family safer and more resilient, you need to understand what
each member faces.

The next step is to identify the specific threats you face for everything
on your list.

What's a threat?

In every activity, at every location, for any kind of transportation, you
face identifiable danger of some sort. We're going to refer to any mani-
festation of any danger as a "threat."

It's easy to get into the habit of thinking of threats as being only criminals or terrorists, but you need to broaden your thinking: A threat is
any person, object or event that places you or a loved one in danger of

death, severe injury, or significant alteration of your life as you know it today. Anything that is likely to negatively impact your future is a threat.

With that definition in mind, what threats do you face in your life? Of course everyone always thinks of the bad people — the evil people — and when I say "self-defense," most people conjure up rapists and muggers. But it goes much deeper than that.

Fire, for instance, is always a threat, whether you're at home, in a restaurant, or out camping. In fact, I once had to evacuate a long-term camp in a wilderness area due to a massive forest fire. Auto crashes are certainly a threat, as are workplace accidents, pedestrian-automobile encounters, natural disasters, and even manmade disasters. Consider all the dangers you're exposed to as threats to your life and well-being.

What about the threat of a job loss or severe economic downturn? What if a drought happened in your part of the country? Have you thought about an accident that closes the only road into your town for a couple of weeks? A month-long power outage? All you need to do is watch the news to discover these are all things that have happened somewhere in this country just in the last year.

How about having your gas main, electrical service, or water cut off during a major storm? (My wife and I have had to deal with widespread week-long power outages, in the middle of winter, twice in our lifetimes — once when we were living in one of the most affluent cities in our state.) Has your car ever broken down on a desolate road? Have you ever come close to a traumatic injury due to either your job or any of your hobbies? These are all threats.

Finally, health issues are a big threat for many people. They can severely alter your future just as surely as a car accident or a mugger's bullet. Many health issues are under your control, but even those that aren't can be prepared for. You prepare to lessen the long-term impacts, and that can be done for a severe illness just as it can for a flood.

Moderation is a virtue

People display two common tendencies when doing this sort of threat assessment. The first is downplaying the extent or the impact of the dangers in their lives. This leads to a failure to identify their actual threats and results in gaps in their preparedness. It's very easy to think something won't affect you, and even easier to think you're more prepared than you really are to face that threat.

The second is going overboard, by identifying threats that either aren't likely to happen or by confusing real dangers with mere inconveniences that don't significantly impact their health or well-being. If you're an optimist by nature, you'll tend toward the former. If you're a born pessimist like me, you'll probably be more like the latter!

I've given you numerous examples of potential threats, but remember, they're just that: examples. You're unlikely to face all of those, but you might identify threats in your life I haven't listed. It's your life, and only you can decide what is and isn't a danger to your health, safety, and well-being.

Regardless of your life outlook, remember the States of Expectation we covered earlier. Make your list of threats that are plausible rather than merely possible. There needs to be a sufficient history of occurrence that makes it reasonable to assume it could happen to you. Later you'll assign priority to the likely (probable) subset of the threats on your list.

Step Two: Calculating risk

Now that you have your list of threats based on your life (and the lives of your loved ones), it's time to determine your risk: your exposure to the danger the threat represents.

As you've no doubt surmised, even within your list not all the threats you've identified are equal. Some happen more often than others; the more often, the higher the *incidence*. For each threat on your list, decide whether it's of low incidence (doesn't happen often or isn't very likely) or high incidence (happens often or is very likely to happen). Give each a number between 1 and 10; the larger the number, the higher the incidence.

Don't get overly analytical at this stage. This is your personal assessment, not a research paper. At the same time, be realistic: do tsunamis happen all that often in Phoenix?

Once you've done that, consider each threat from the standpoint of the impact it would have on your life. This is called the consequence, and is harder to judge because of the different kinds of impacts: physical, psychological, emotional, and financial. Many threats involve more than one of those impacts, and each has a different combination of impacts and severity.

Considering all the impacts any specific threat might have on your life, give each threat a number between 1 and 10. The higher the number, the higher the negative impact on your life. Consequence is even more subjective than incidence, as each person has a very different view of severity. Some people may rank psychological effects above physical impacts, while others may consider a risk of death, even if very small, to be their overriding concern. I'm not going to tell you how to assess the impact on your life, because your life is your own to live. I'm simply asking you to assign a number to how high the consequence is to you.

You now have two numbers for each threat — incidence and consequence. Multiply them to come up with a single number for each threat. We'll call this the "Risk Index," and it represents a relative measure of the threat to your life. It serves as a rough indicator of how important that threat is in your self-protection plan.

How big is the number?

It's very unusual for someone living in the United States to be exposed to threats that are both highest in incidence and highest in consequence. We have a relatively ordered society compared to some places on earth, so unless you and/or your circumstances are very unusual, you probably won't have any threats that rate a "100"!

On the other hand, if you have identified threats that rate a "2," you probably don't need to worry too much about preparing for those.

This process of threat assessment should, if you've been both thorough and realistic, result in a rough game plan: You know what you need to deal with and how important each is. The next step is to decide what you'll do first.

When it comes to personal security, family safety, and home protection preparation, sometimes getting started is the hard part. That's why I had you do the threat assessment exercise, because the results help you decide where to start. That assessment helps guide your self-protection plan, so you know what to do first.

The Risk Index gives you a rough idea how much of your resources (time, energy, money, and interest) you should spend on preparing for each threat.

"It's not the odds, it's the stakes"

Some people, particularly in the world of defensive shooting, will tell you that you absolutely need to subscribe to their way of doing things because "it's not the odds, it's the stakes."

Actually, it's both.

Let's take the saying to its logical conclusion: Being hit by a sufficiently large meteorite would no doubt prove instantly fatal. Why not prepare for that? Why not spend the time and money to install an observatory in your house and constantly scan the sky looking for the telltale signs of a large rock coming toward you? Why not build your home deep underground, safe from all but extinction-level impacts? Perhaps armor the roof of your car? Radar installation, anyone?

No one does any of that, because the chance of being killed by a meteorite strike is absurdly remote. In fact, in the entire recorded history of man, no human being has been scientifically verified to have been killed by a meteorite.* It would appear not to be *just* the stakes, after all!

Your risk profile is a combination of both the odds (incidence) and the stakes (consequence) for any given threat. Many dangers could result in your death, but not all of them are preventable or avoidable. It's not worth your time or effort to worry about those.

Even preventable or avoidable events are not all equal. Some have higher odds than others, and some are easier to prepare for.

We come back to the hard truth that you simply can't prepare for everything. When it comes right down to it, it's neither the odds nor the stakes. It's a combination of both, and part of your planning requires you to make decisions about how you'll value each. That decision needs to be made for each identified threat.

In some cases, you may decide the low-probability, high-impact event is more important than one that is more likely to occur but has slightly less consequence. That's fine, but understand why you're making the decision and don't live your life by someone else's soundbite.

Self-protection plan: by the numbers

If you've completed the threat assessment — identifying and ranking the dangers you might face in your life — you now have numbers associated with each of them. By ranking them by both incidence (how common they are) and consequence (the amount of effect they have on your life), then multiplying those numbers, you end up with a Risk Index figure that gives you some guidance as to the importance of preparing for that threat.

What do I mean by the importance of any given threat? You can think of it in two ways: First, how much of your preparation resources you choose (or perhaps should choose) to devote to it, always with the understanding that those resources are limited. Second, how urgently you should prepare.

Deciding how to allocate your scarce resources

You're probably tired of me saying this, but it needs to be repeated: Your preparedness resources are limited. No one has unlimited money, energy, interest, or — especially — time to train, equip, and practice for every possible thing that could happen to them. The resources you spend learning how to defend yourself with a firearm can't be spent learning how to home-can food or how to deal with severe life-threatening trauma.

Even within each category you might need to make resource decisions in your self-protection plan. Let's take self-defense shooting: You need shooting skills and knowledge, but you also need to know when it's appropriate to use those skills — the legal part of the equation. If you've allocated some amount of your preparedness resources to learn how to defend yourself with a firearm, you need to decide how much of that goes to a shooting class and how much to a law class.

(Hint: Most people don't even bother with the latter, because the former is a lot more fun! Some of them wish they'd made a different decision when they wind up in jail for using their gun inappropriately.)

The higher the Risk Index, the larger the percentage of your preparedness resources you might want to spend on planning for that specific threat.

Prioritizing by urgency

Which threat should you prepare for first? Numbers alone don't tell the whole story, and you may find an item that has a slightly lower Risk Index than another threat, yet you feel it's more important to prepare for. Even if two threats have the same numerical value, you might decide to do one before the other because you feel a compelling reason.

This brings up an important point: Don't be a slave to the numbers. It's easy to get overly fixated on rankings when doing this exercise, but you may find your gut telling you to prepare for a "lesser" threat, numerically speaking, than one that ranks higher. Sometimes this is a sign that you've overstated or understated something when you did your initial rankings. If so, be honest with yourself. Go back and re-rank those items to more accurately reflect your assessment of their incidence and consequence. Your self-protection plan is first and foremost about *you*.

Even if after re-evaluation, you truly believe the rankings to be perfectly valid, you may still feel a desire to prepare for one before you tackle another. That's perfectly fine — as long as your feelings aren't driven by the entertainment or pleasure value of the activity.

For instance, shooting is (for a lot of people) a fun activity, and taking a shooting class is even more fun. For some, there is entertainment value in getting out and playing soldier or SWAT cop for a weekend. But don't let your enjoyment of the activity blind you to its actual preparedness value or lack thereof.

In reality, the majority of defensive gun uses are relatively mundane and undemanding of shooting skill, but almost all are very demanding of judgement and self-control. Learning how to shoot doesn't usually do much for learning how to process information. If you use your resources having fun while skipping out on what actually keeps you safe, have you made the best of your limited time, energy, and money?

Be honest with yourself: separate preparedness and entertainment.

This doesn't mean preparedness can't be fun or enjoyable, but if that's all it is, it probably isn't making you safer.

Prioritizing by commonalities

At the beginning of this book, you read about opportunity cost and how it applies to your self-protection. It suggests you consider losses in other areas of preparedness when making a decision about how you'll equip and train in one area. Opportunity cost applies when choosing between mutually exclusive alternatives.

As it happens, mutual exclusivity is not absolute in your personal security. As you've learned, there is likely to be some overlap in the various aspects of your self-protection plan (or there can be with some slight alterations). For example, the work you do to prevent residential burglary will also often reduce the chances of a successful home invasion — and vice-versa. Preparing for severe weather? That's a lot like preparing for being stranded away from home (and the former is often the reason for the latter).

Many of the threats you face can be affected by preparations you've made for another. Two (or more) of your threats might use the same set of Respond resources, or be Deterred by the same environmental changes. When you look at your planning beyond the single threat you're considering, you might find some overlap — overlap that pushes that particular preparation higher in priority, even if the Risk Index says the individual threats by themselves aren't terribly important.

Things that do dual (or triple) duty are more efficient and should be given preparedness priority over things that are less efficient (unique or limited in scope).

What about the other family members?

Keep in mind the numbers you have are for you, but might not be accurate for everyone. If you re-run the exercise for other members of your family, you might find them shifting a bit. For instance, abduction attempts occur with children far more than they do with adults, and the preparedness resources you spend on your kids might change to reflect that reality. I encourage you to do this risk assessment process for each family member and integrate that information into your planning.

Now all you have to do is decide how much time, effort, and money you have to budget for each item in your self-protection plan, then get started!

Making threat assessment easy

To make this easier for you, I've prepared a printable Threat Assessment worksheet you can download and fill out. It's part of my Prepping For Life Worksheet Pack, and includes the Preparedness Inventory mentioned earlier along with the Matrix form you'll need in the next chapter. If you have a spreadsheet app on your computer or tablet, I've included an Excel spreadsheet version which eliminates the math and allows you to sort your threats by any criteria you choose.

www.getgrant.us/prepping

(* According to NASA, the much-publicized 2016 death in India was the result of a land-based explosion, not a meteorite:

www.nytimes.com/2016/02/10/world/asia/that-wasnt-a-meteorite-that-killed-a-man-in-india-nasa-says.html)

THE ADAPTIVE PERSONAL SECURITY MATRIX

The Adaptive Personal Security approach uses a simple three-by-three matrix to help you identify and track your preparedness progress. This matrix makes it easy to see where you're prepared and where you might need to place more emphasis. It shows you graphically how close to balance you are in any area.

Each plausible threat you've identified gets its own matrix. On the top are the three structural functions of Deter, Detect, and Respond. On the side are the actionable activities of Equip, Train, and Maintain.

Think of the matrix as both a planner and a diary. It helps you see what you need to do today and tomorrow, as well as showing what you did yesterday. Here's an overview of how it works. The specifics of each item are detailed in following chapters.

How the matrix works

Start by labeling the matrix with the specific plausible threat you're preparing for. Don't generalize here; be specific. If you've identified burglaries of your house as a threat, don't put "home security"; use "home burglaries."

Next, identify the base effect of that threat. Drill down and find the underlying reason you need to be concerned about that threat. For example, if the threat is wildfire, why is it a problem? Because your house might catch on fire. Why is that a problem? Because your house might be destroyed. Why is that a problem? Because you'll have no shelter for a long period of time while you rebuild (if you even can). That's the base effect of wildfire and the real reason you're preparing against it.

After you've figured out the base effect, ask yourself what the worst-case scenario of that threat would be. While you do this, remember that the worst-case scenario is the worst case you're likely to experience, not necessarily the worst case that could possibly happen. Back to my earthquake example: the worst-case scenario is the massive subduction zone quake that not only destroys my house, but also those around me and the surrounding local infrastructure, which we'd normally turn to for temporary shelter and recovery efforts. That's what I'd write down.

The base effect allows you to compare activities over different threats. It's easy to think of two threats as unrelated, but when you see you've identified the same (or very similar) base effects, it's easier to coordinate your activities to avoid duplication or wasted effort. This is one of the big "secrets" that makes the adaptive approach work so well.

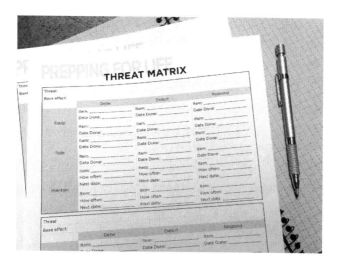

Down to specifics

Now look at the intersection of the first function (Deter) and the first activity (Equip). What is the most effective tool, device, or feature you can acquire, make, or install that will keep that threat from coming into contact with or affecting you?

Let's say the threat you're working on is a home-invasion burglar. The best Deterrence might be better locksets and deadbolts to keep him from making entry. Write that down. Note there are two lines: What's the next most effective thing you might do to keep that home invader from coming into contact with you? You might decide that motion-sensing lights would scare him off (as they often do). If so, write those down.

If you can't think of a second item or activity, don't worry. There might not be two things, or you might think of something else later. If you've already done the most important thing or things, write those down and mark them as "done." The Adaptive Personal Security approach allows you to see what you've done as well as what you need to do!

Move down to the next empty cell in the matrix: Train. What skills might you need to Deter that threat? Write that skill or skills down. Again, if you already feel you possess those, write them down and mark them as done by entering the date. That's one less thing you need to worry about doing!

Finally, move down to the Maintain activity. What do you need to do to maintain the tools and skills you've identified? For every tool, you generally need to do something to keep it in working order. For instance, a firearm needs cleaning and lubrication on a regular basis, even if it's not used. Your shooting skills need regular practice to maintain them in a usable state. Even something as mundane as an evacuation plan needs the occasional drill to make sure you remember what to do, when to do it, and how it should be done.

When you put something in the Maintain activity, decide how often it needs to be done and then commit to doing it. Maintenance might be regular practice, a Response drill, or cleaning and keeping a piece of equipment in operable condition. Whatever you're doing to maintain that item, write down when you're going to do it. That might be weekly, monthly, quarterly, or even yearly depending on the item, but make sure to enter it.

Put a corresponding entry in your personal planner or calendar. Once you've done that, you can check the "Scheduled" box in the matrix.

After you've finished the Deter column for the specific threat, move over and do the same things for the Detect and Respond functions. When you're finished with the matrix, you should ideally have at least one item in each cell. Some of them may already be marked as done, which means you don't need to waste time and energy on them — you can allocate your scarce preparedness resources to something else on your list. When you've finished with the matrix for a specific threat, you'll be able to see what you've already done and what you still need to do.

When you have all the cells filled in, you know your planning is balanced; when each of the cells has a check, you know your implementation is balanced. For that threat, you can rest assured you've done your best to prepare! Do the same for the rest of the threats you face.

Keeping track of duplication

Since some preparedness activities are applicable to multiple threats, you may find yourself making entries in several different matrixes simultaneously. Things that are effective against the home burglar may also be effective against the home-invasion criminal. Things that protect you from muggings may also be effective for carjackings. It's rare to have 100% overlap between threats, but you may find several activities common to two (or more) threats.

This is one of the benefits of the Adaptive Personal Security approach, and particularly the activity of identifying the base effect of the threat. Discovering where your preparedness overlaps lets you make progress more efficiently by leveraging the effects of each of your activities.

Leveraging your preparedness activities is a powerful way to make the best use of your limited preparedness resources. It's easy, even for those of us who are deeply into the preparedness lifestyle, to lose track of where we are with regard to our overall personal security. I did, and the Adaptive Personal Security matrix was the single most powerful thing I found to help me make intelligent preparations for my safety and that of my family.

By looking at the matrixes, you can quickly see where your preparedness activities are really paying off. You can see where you're most efficient and see just how small preparedness activities can make a big difference in your personal and family safety.

Balance, peace, and accomplishment

One of the reasons personal planning systems are such powerful motivators is because they allow you to see not only what you need to do, but just as importantly what you've already done. There's a huge motivational value to seeing what you've accomplished at the end of the day, and every time you check off something on your daily to-do list, you get a little shot of dopamine that makes you feel good at having done so.

The Adaptive Personal Security matrix is the same thing, but for your preparedness. A comforting feeling comes over me whenever I see a matrix that's been filled in, and again as I watch the "done" checkmarks populate each cell. It's a combination of pride in accomplishment and the peace of mind that comes from knowing I've done something to make myself and my family safer and more resilient.

I keep coming back to the idea of balance because it's so important to your motivation and commitment. Seeing the balance happen before your eyes in the form of your filled preparedness matrixes is a powerful visual reminder of the peace that comes from personal security. The balance between what you need to do and what you know you can do is laid before you in a form you can easily see and understand.

The matrix form

You don't need anything elaborate or fancy to make your own matrix forms. You can even hand-draw them on the pages of your daily journal, so they're always handy! That didn't work out so well for me, though, because I can't draw a straight line with a ruler. So I made my own forms, and you can use them too!

My free downloadable Worksheet Pack has the Matrix form, along with the Preparedness Inventory and Threat Assessment worksheets you already know about. You can get them all at this link:

www.getgrant.us/prepping

You can also make a suitable form in a spreadsheet or word processor.

Whether you prefer to fill yours out by hand or on your computer, it's vitally important to print out your matrixes. Keep them handy so you can review them from time to time. The visual representation is a powerful motivational tool both to keep you on your preparedness track and to remind you how well prepared you are. Both go a long way toward helping you achieve the peace you set out to acquire!

THE 80% SOLUTION

You're going to get tired of me saying this, but it's crucial to keeping on track with your preparedness: You can't prepare for everything possible, because you don't have the unlimited resources it would take to do so. You only have so much time, energy, money, and interest to spend on your preparedness, and you need to make sure those resources are used on the most important things.

Just as it's not possible to prepare for everything, it's not possible to prepare perfectly for any one thing. How do you know when you're getting optimum value from your investment of preparedness resources?

The Pareto Principle

Back in 1896, an Italian economist named Vilfredo Pareto made an interesting and far-reaching observation: 80% of the pea harvest in his garden came from a mere 20% of his peapods. He later discovered the same proportions applied to land ownership: 80% of the property in his native Italy was owned by 20% of the population. The Pareto Principle has since been shown to be a fairly accurate predictor in many other fields and has come to represent the most efficient use of resources.

The real lesson Pareto taught us is often lost. For each point of result above 80%, you have to spend a correspondingly larger amount of your resources. To get an 80% satisfactory result, you spend 20% of your time/money/effort/interest. But to reach just the 90% mark might cost you 70% or 85% of your resources.

It's easy to get lost in the numbers, and of course the exact percentages vary depending on exactly what we're talking about, but the point is, once you get past that first 80%, your use of resources goes up out of all proportion to the result you actually achieve. Getting to 80% is very efficient, but after that, efficiency drops off very rapidly. For every percent of your resources you spend after that point, you get less and less return.

Long-range shooters understand this. Building a precision rifle costs money, and each small increment of precision you seek costs proportionally more. You can buy any number of rifles off-the-shelf that will deliver superb results for most shooters, but if you want one even just a little better, the price triples or quadruples. The "sweet spot" is where price and performance are at that shooter's 80% level, because anything above that costs a lot more money.

Applying Pareto to preparedness

I believe it's useful to figure out what the 80% solution is for each of your preparedness activities, and resolve to get to that point for all of them before trying to refine any one.

Being 80% prepared for everything is, in my opinion, much better than spending all your resources trying to get to 95% on one or two things. The latter leaves gaps in your preparedness and, in my mind, doesn't make you that much safer.

I see this all the time in defensive shooting students. I've run across many who spend inordinate amounts of money each year on training classes, new guns and gear, and ammunition — but who haven't managed to put together decent medical kits or developed an evacuation plan for their family. They have lots of bullets, but no backstock of food for an emergency. They've spent all their discretionary resources on guns and shooting, which they're substantially less likely to need than good locks on their doors.

Don't take this to mean you should never seek to be better prepared. You may decide the Risk Index for any given threat justifies a greater-than-80% solution, and that's fine. Just don't let your pursuit of 90% or 95% suck up resources that are needed to prepare for the other high-index threats on your list. When you've reached the 80% solution for all the important threats, you can go back and selectively decide where you'll spend more resources to get a higher level of protection.

But remember that your expenditures go way up for each small increase above 80% in your preparedness level — and you still won't be completely protected. There is no such thing as a risk-free life; you never reach 100% preparedness. A large part of achieving the all-important balance in your preparedness is accepting that fact. Do what you can, be happy with the result, and move on to the next item on your list.

I recommend aiming for the 80% solution on all your preparations before you dive deeper into any one item.

A DIFFERENT PERSPECTIVE ON RISK

Before we get too deeply into the planning and execution phases, I think it's important to take a step back and look at the bigger picture. Some people call this the "40,000 foot view," and it should give you some perspective on what's really important in your life.

This may be uncomfortable to read, but if you're intellectually honest, you need to. Please be aware that I'm not here to throw stones at you. Of the people in my circle, I can't think of any who aren't impacted by at least some of what we'll discuss here. In other words, no one is perfect, and I'm certainly not pretending I am! But if you're serious about protecting your own life, you owe it to yourself and your family to face up to these issues and start fixing them first.

Why are you really reading this book?

We're all afraid of dying. That is, I suspect, a lot of the motivation behind self-defense and personal-security preparedness. I don't want my life to end prematurely, and I strongly suspect you're the same way!

That's probably why you're reading this book. You want to know what you can do to protect your life, and by extension the lives of your loved ones, so you don't die before you can live a full and happy life. Figuring out the risks you face, the threat they pose to your life, and taking steps to mitigate those risks are rational ways to approach the problem.

But I'm willing to bet that every day you studiously ignore some risks that are quite threatening yet very much within your span of control — even without planning and preparation. This chapter is where we look at those.

Statistical food for thought

In this country, homicide (a small percentage of which are justifiable, but the bulk are criminal) claims around 16,000 people per year. Fires of all kinds account for over 3,000 fatalities a year. Floods, on average, kill about 85 people annually; hurricanes, around 40; tornadoes account for nearly 100; severe heat over 100, severe cold about 30, and a bit more than 50 die each year from non-specific high-wind events.

These are all things we commonly prepare for. When you do your threat assessment, you'll no doubt list events that could result in one of these kinds of deaths. But most of these are outside your control. Of course you can control how prepared you are to deal with them, but in most cases, the actual cause is something well outside your span of influence.

Now let's look at some statistics about events over which you *do* have a great deal of control.

In the United States, 360,000 people die each year of causes directly related to uncontrolled blood pressure. Obesity-related conditions account for another 300,000. Smoking kills an astonishing 480,000 people a year in this country, and alcohol claims another 88,000 — and that doesn't count the nearly 10,000 who die from auto accidents in which alcohol was involved.

You may be in more danger than you're willing to acknowledge.

Facing your demons

In my self-defense and preparedness classes, I've had students who were noticeably overweight, and many more who had a smoking habit. I've even known a few self-defense instructors who fit both descriptions. Many people add in a potential alcohol problem for a triple whammy of risk.

Each of them spent lots of time and money on guns and shooting classes, ostensibly to increase their lifespan by preventing a bad guy from killing them. In the meantime, they were blissfully unconcerned that their chosen lifestyles were killing them far more reliably and predictably than any home invader. Statistically, they were very unlikely to ever see the need to protect themselves from a criminal before the almost inevitable heart attack killed them.

Again, I'm not here to throw stones. I suffer from a bit of a weight problem myself, one that my doctor reminds me can lead to heart issues and diabetes. I take that threat more seriously than anything else I do, and I'll admit it's a tough thing to battle. I understand the challenge!

At the same time, it's important for both of us to understand that the things that are most under our control are by far the most likely to actually kill us. I'm not saying you shouldn't prepare for tornadoes in tornado country, or in my case earthquakes in an earthquake zone, only that we should both consider starting a lot closer to home.

The reality is that taking care of yourself has orders of magnitude more positive impact on your lifespan than the number of guns you have stashed around the house. Before you take yet another self-defense class or start stockpiling ammunition, consider fixing the issues you have with your physical health. The return on your effort is likely to be far greater.

Make your health part of your planning

If you have issues that affect your long-term personal safety, don't shy away from tackling them as part of your overall security planning. Be open with yourself: add the item(s) to your planning and work on it/them just as you would any of the other threats you've identified. This helps take away any stigma or self-imposed guilt you might feel, by making it merely one of a number of personal preparedness steps you're taking. By planning how to mitigate that threat, you also give yourself an action outline and the motivation to do the work necessary to address it.

I've found that seeing my own health as a vital part of my long-term preparedness helps me avoid the natural weekly or monthly variances in my progress. That, in turn, allows me to focus on my long-term progress and see that I'm better today than last year, and the year before. Progress may be slow, but it's always forward!

Sources:

Homicide: www.cdc.gov/nchs/fastats/homicide.htm

Weather: www.nws.noaa.gov/om/hazstats/resources/weather_fatalities.pdf

Fire: www.usfa.fema.gov/data/statistics/

Hypertension: www.cdc.gov/bloodpressure/facts.htm

Obesity: wvdhhr.org/bph/oehp/obesity/mortality.htm

Smoking: www.cdc.gov/tobacco/data_statistics/fact_sheets/fast_facts/

Alcohol: www.niaaa.nih.gov/alcohol-health/overview-alcohol-consumption/alcohol-facts-and-statistics

EQUIP

I'll start with an acknowledgement: yes, you need some gear. You should have the best gear you can afford. With that acknowledgement, however, comes a caution: you probably don't need a lot of it. Certainly not as much as some people would have you believe!

Consumerism run amok?

It's easy, perhaps too easy, to get caught up in buying gear. Our society has conditioned us to believe that if we have a problem, buying something will solve the problem. In self-defense, a very large percentage of people believe buying a gun will make them safe. Even if they say they don't believe it, their spending patterns usually tell a different story. It's almost considered a virtue to be fixated on the gear. Note I said "almost"!

The core of the Adaptive Personal Security approach is to view your self-protection as a whole; to be flexible and bring all your appropriate preparedness resources to bear on any given problem. But a hardware orientation tends to make you less flexible. Gear focuses your

Response, in the way that having only a hammer makes all your problems look like nails.

Gear also eats up a substantial portion of your preparedness budget. Good gear isn't usually cheap, and buying lots of it means you have that much less to spend on other things — like the training to use it. As an example, I've run into people with multiple safes full of guns who wouldn't take a defensive shooting class because it was "too expensive." (My response? "Sell a gun and take a class." By their facial expressions, you'd think I'd committed some sort of heresy!) That's what happens when you let yourself become fixated on the gear.

Buy what you need, not what society has conditioned you to want.

Watch out for "gear porn"

A whole genre of social media is devoted to "gear porn": attractive pictures of guns and knives and vehicles and clothing you simply must have. Some are honest about the visceral appeal and make no apologies for the conspicuous consumption aspects.

If you want to be truly prepared, do your best to avoid gear porn purveyors.

I admit it's fun to look at pictures of the stuff other people own and aspire to owning it yourself. I've occasionally fallen into that trap. When I've succumbed, I always found ways to justify the purchase to myself. Later, in the cold light of day, I discovered that my rationalizations didn't really fit my plans.

Let your plan be your guide to what you buy. Acquire gear that will help you, and avoid wasting your resources on items just to satisfy your acquisitive nature.

"Two is one, and one is none" *

One common justification people use to explain their uncontrolled acquisitiveness goes to the idea of redundancy: If you want to be truly safe, you need backups for all critical equipment.

There is some merit to this idea. It stems from the observation that if you have only one piece of critical equipment and it breaks, you're left with nothing but your wits. It comes to us courtesy of the military, where backup plans and gear are a way of life.

Of course, the military has the budget, storage facilities, transportation capabilities, and maintenance crews to support redundancy. You and I don't.

It's prudent to have some form of redundancy for the most critical parts of your preparations, but that doesn't necessarily mean duplicates. It might mean a multipurpose item that can double as several other items, or it might mean a completely different way of dealing with the problem altogether.

For instance, power outages are common in many rural areas. A generator is a prudent way of responding to those events, but the generators themselves are somewhat complex and have multiple failure points. What if the generator runs out of fuel or breaks down? Shouldn't you have two of them? Given the cost of a good generator capable of running a household, that would be economically prohibitive for most people.

Instead, think of the generator not as providing electricity, but rather facilitating things such as light, heat, and cooked food. When you think in those terms, you realize they can be provided by other means, such as solar-charged flashlights, woodstoves, and camping stoves. Those can be the backup for the generator (and serve as preparedness for other kinds of events as well).

Let the problem and the job to be done determine whether you need redundancy and what those backup systems should consist of. Drill down to the core: The job of the generator isn't to provide electricity — it's to give you light, heat, and cooking capabilities. Think of it that way and it's easy to come up with alternatives.

If the solution to the problem has multiple points of failure, and the need for that solution is frequent, consider alternative ways of achieving the same result. Only in the most extreme cases do you need backups for your backups.

What do you really need?

In a theoretically ideal world, you'd avoid ever getting to the point that a Response is necessary. Safety isn't the ability to save yourself or get out of danger when it manifests itself (the Respond phase of the framework). Instead safety comes from not needing to face the threat in the first place, which is where the protective functions of Deter and Detect come into play.

Hardware used in the Deter and Detect phases will likely address multiple threats and scenarios, as opposed to the often task-specific hardware commonly used in the Respond phase. Once you get to Respond, hardware tends to become more specialized and have a narrower range of application.

Take, for instance, a video security system. As a Deterrence device, the presence of visible security cameras may ward off petty thieves, vandals, pranksters, burglars, and home invaders. In the Detect phase, it gives you advance warning of all of those and many other minor annoyances and inconveniences. It also gives you evidence gathering for the Respond phase.

Now contrast that with the home-defense firearm, which is only useful as a Response tool in those cases where you've positively identified a potentially lethal threat. That's a very narrow subset of all the incidents listed above. The video security system does far more for your safety and may in fact prevent you from ever needing to retrieve your home-defense firearm in the first place.

I'm not saying a defensive firearm is useless or that you shouldn't have one. What I am saying is when you consider where to make your first home security purchase, perhaps the video security system is a smarter move than the gun.

How to decide what hardware is necessary

Look back to your threat assessment and think about the dangers you've identified. Take them one at a time and ask yourself what gear or hardware you need to protect yourself from the threat (that is, to Deter and Detect), then ask what you'd need to Respond to the threat in the worst-case scenario. A hardware investment in the Deter and Detect phases might give you a higher return on your safety investment than if it were spent on the more limited Respond phase, particularly if the gear addresses more than one threat (which is likely in those phases of the framework).

Once you've identified a potential hardware purchase, ask yourself what you expect it to do. If alternatives exist that would address the same threat but are cheaper, more reliable, more readily available, have additional benefits, or require less ongoing support, they might be a better choice. For example, an alarm system might be a good investment — but a dog with a loud bark might be just as effective in the alert role, as well as providing a healthy dose of Deterrence. Besides, you can't hug an alarm system (and it can't take you for regular walks, which will improve your health and fitness and thereby increase your overall preparedness.)

Look at the expected frequency of use and the consequences of failure. Is it prudent to have some sort of backup or redundancy capability? Backup doesn't necessarily mean "identical," but most certainly means being able to address the threat in some way that will make you safer.

Ask yourself, "What is the opportunity cost of this item? What will I give up by buying it?" Remember, you don't have unlimited resources. What you spend on this item you can't spend on something else. Is it really that important? Perhaps some cost cutting would lower your opportunity cost without reducing your preparedness in any significant way.

Be sure to factor in the ongoing maintenance of the hardware — and I'm not just talking about oil changes and alignments! Some items require more ongoing training and practice than others. When I recommend firearms for personal defense, I recommend those that are the most efficient — i.e., those that require the fewest motions and manipulations to bring to a ready-to-fire state. Some firearms are objectively less efficient than others, but this doesn't mean they can't be used for self-defense. However, it does mean the ongoing maintenance costs in practice and training are higher than the more efficient choices.

Don't just buy, and don't just buy because someone else bought. To achieve balance in your personal security, think through your purchases carefully and always aim to get the most for your investment of preparedness resources.

A minimalist approach

As noted above, there is a tendency to over-prepare in some areas while neglecting others. This is especially true with gear, because gear is cool. It's tangible. You can show it off to your friends, and then they have a motivation to one-up you by acquiring more or "better" gear. Then you're motivated to outdo them, and preparedness turns into a vicious cycle of consumerism.

Paying attention to your balance, what you need to do and what you can do, is the first step to counteracting this acquisition bug. Once you've gotten to the point of enough — addressing the threat in all four phases — just stop. Spend your money on something else. When you've addressed all the threats on your list, go for a hike or play tennis. Enjoy the peace that comes from the balance you've earned.

While you do need some gear, skill and knowledge are even more important than the hardware you buy. They're easier to store and are far more portable, and they're applicable over a wider range of circumstances. If the choice is between what goes into your head and what goes into your garage, start with your head. Learn, practice, and then augment with the gear you need as opposed to the gear you want. Let your head tell you what to put in your garage, not the other way around.

(* — *A bit of humor: If two is really one, if you have two items you really only have one — and as we've been told, one is none. Therefore, two is none because one is none and two is only one, which is none. That means you probably need three. But three is just two plus one, and since two is one, you only have one plus one. Since one is none, one plus one is really none plus none, which is none. So even three is really none. See how silly some of these meaningless sayings can be when taken to their conclusion?*)

TRAIN

One of the overlooked aspects of personal security is training, which is common in the self-defense world, but becomes less and less common as you move away from that field. And yet training — learning new skills specific to an activity — is vitally important in being able to put your plans into action.

It's not enough to own good gear. You have to know how to use it. Even some relatively mundane tasks will produce better results if you've been taught how to do them properly.

Training examples

Let's take defensive shooting as an example, because it's a field where I have a significant amount of training time both as a student and a teacher. The majority of people who buy guns for self or home protection never take a course in how to use them in self-defense. Many people think that, because they were in the military or their uncle is a retired cop, they know all they need to use their gun in a self-defense situation.

In reality they don't. Self-defense in the private sector is very different than military activity or even law enforcement. The situations under which the firearm is used, how it's used, and when it's allowed to be used are very different. Many people never learn how to use their firearm efficiently against a surprise threat — the kind of threat we in the private sector almost always face. They don't understand the legalities of the use of lethal force, and as a result many see the inside of a jail cell for shooting someone they shouldn't.

Even a simple thing like storing the gun responsibly seems to be foreign to a lot of people!

The firearm is, in one sense, an easy thing to use: pull the trigger, and the gun goes "bang." Using it properly, judiciously, and safely is neither intuitive nor easy, which is where training comes in.

Training isn't just about firearms

If you intend to carry a trauma kit to deal with life-threatening injuries, you need to know how to use it properly. That's where training under a knowledgeable and experienced instructor comes in. It might make the difference between a life saved and one made worse by ignorant intervention.

If you have a chainsaw for clearing downed trees after a storm, where did you learn to use it? A chainsaw is an incredibly dangerous tool, as illustrated by the over 30,000 severe injuries every year in this country. The average chainsaw injury requires a whopping 110 stitches!* Isn't it a good idea to have someone teach you how to use your chainsaw properly before you're thrust into a situation where you need it — and where emergency medical care might be delayed or even unavailable?

Many other activities related to preparedness and personal security benefit from professional training. Sometimes training is a matter of efficiency, saving you the time of figuring it out yourself and increasing the quality of your results. Other times it's a matter of safety — yours or someone else's. The key is knowing when training is prudent and when it's not really needed, then getting the amount of training necessary without investing an inordinate amount of resources.

Thoughts on training

Some might consider this chapter a little self-serving, as one of the things I do is to teach people certain skills. While I'm a proponent of training, keep in mind that some things can be self-taught. The definition of training I use is learning a new skill. Never did I say it always has to be from someone else.

In general, anything dealing with safety issues — defensive shooting is a really good example — should be done through a professional, hands-on course. Many other things you can learn on your own, at your own pace.

Don't be a training junkie

Taking a class is a lot of fun, particularly when you get to do things like shoot guns. But many people tend to take more and more fun classes and justify them as being preparedness planning.

I see this often in the defensive shooting world. I teach all over the country, and a large percentage of my students have already trained with someone else. Many of them take more than one shooting class every year, and a surprisingly large percentage have attended classes from more than a half-dozen "big name" instructors. Training is their hobby, their recreation, and I don't mean to imply there's anything wrong with that.

But going back to our understanding of training resources, if you're taking two or three shooting classes a year, are you really any better prepared? A good training class is expensive. Add in ammunition, travel, lodging, and meals and it can reach a sizable sum of money. Factor in your time, energy, and interest, and it's a substantial chunk out of your limited preparation resources.

It's easy to get drawn into training for any kind of preparedness skill and allocate resources out of all proportion to the value received. If you choose to have a defensive firearm, you certainly need to know how to use it safely and efficiently, as well as understanding the complex legal world of lethal force. But once you've taken those classes, will another class make you better prepared?

I submit that your preparedness resources might be better spent practicing and maintaining the skills you learned in class, and apportioning the rest of your resources to make preparations for the other threats you face. This is why the threat matrixes you filled out earlier are so important. They keep you on track and prevent you from spending your resources frivolously. After you have taken defensive firearms training and have committed to a practice and maintenance regimen, it's time to focus on preparedness activities for other threats.

Train relevant skills

Always ask yourself, "Is what I'm training really relevant to my life and the threats I face?"

In a way, this question relates to the training junkie topic. In their search for ever-more-exciting training, many people will start to drift in their assessment of what's necessary. After a while, they're taking courses in shooting from hovering helicopters because they've concocted a fantasy future where they need to do that. (No, I am not kidding. Schools exist that will give you this opportunity.)

Is shooting from a helicopter really important to your preparedness? Where does it fit into your threat matrixes? It probably doesn't, which makes it irrelevant to what you're doing. Again, if you're labeling it as recreation, I have no quarrel — but be honest with yourself. If it's not relevant, it shouldn't be using up your limited preparedness resources.

Be ruthless in asking the question. If the skill isn't relevant, in big ways or small, don't bother with it.

* — *Source: www.americantreeservicesupply.com/did-you-know*

MAINTAIN

After decades in the fields of personal security, preparedness, and self-defense, I'm still amazed how many people make elaborate plans for their safety and yet never practice their skills. Almost anything you do with regard to protecting yourself and your family needs to be tested and practiced — maintained — to make sure it will actually do the job asked when the time comes. Practice means to maintain your skills and gear so they're always ready to work when they're really needed.

The fire-drill lesson

I don't know how things are in schools these days, but when I was a kid we had regular fire drills. We were taught what to do and where to go in the event of a fire, and every so often we'd practice those procedures to make sure we could get out of the building as quickly and orderly as we could. In addition, the Principal would occasionally sound the fire sirens unexpectedly, so we could experience the sudden need to evacuate the building under somewhat realistic conditions.

(One time in grade school, I happened to be standing directly under one of the sirens when it went off. I can still recall the exact pitch and volume, and my ears rang for a couple of days afterward. More importantly, I also remember the exact route I took to get out of the building safely!)

There is a direct corollary to your home life: your family, too, needs to have a fire evacuation plan. Each member should know exactly where to go and what to do in the case of a fire, and your family needs to occasionally have a fire drill to practice those skills. Of all the people I've talked to about this subject, only a few actually had a fire evacuation plan for their home and practiced it. Does it surprise you that they were teachers?

Beyond the fire

Fire drills aren't just for fires, however. Drills and tests need to be a part of your planning from the beginning. Practice using your equipment and the skills you gained in your training to be sure your plans will actually work.

Practice takes many forms. With defensive shooting, practice means getting out to the range and doing exercises that duplicate what you learned in your shooting courses. Doing the exercises again, looking for errors and correcting them, helps you maintain your shooting skills.

You can also practice your medical skills by having someone pretend to be injured and you apply the proper treatment. Have a practice tourniquet you can use again and again in these exercises. Being able to apply that tourniquet quickly in a stressful situation is an important part of the skill. Practice ensures that you can.

While we're talking about trauma medicine, it's vital to practice self-care as well. You never know when you might be in an accident — or worse, attacked with a knife or gun — and need to save your own life. Can you apply a tourniquet to yourself using only one hand? How about that pressure dressing?

Practice involves exercising your gear, too. If your disaster plans include a generator (and they should), periodically starting and running the generator to power the same appliances it will in a real emergency is critical. Not only does it verify that the generator is still working, it also verifies you remember how to use it safely. Generators produce huge amounts of power, and since that power is often needed in wet and windy conditions, electrocution is a real hazard. Setting up and using the generator without electrocuting yourself are important skills to practice!

Many people have "bug out bags" or "get home bags" that they plan to use to sustain themselves in the case of a widespread disaster. If you have one, have you ever really practiced with it? Try it some weekend: Simulate the need to walk away from your house or vehicle, relying only on your kit for sustenance and shelter. Cut the power in your home or walk out into your yard and stay there for the weekend, subsisting only on what's in your emergency stockpiles or packed bags. I'll bet you find some significant flaws with what you're carrying, your ability to carry it, and/or your skills in using it.

I can't overemphasize the need for practice and testing your preparedness plans. Build practice and testing exercises into your planning from the start.

Practice uses resources

A couple of years ago, our community voted on a new tax levy to maintain our fire district and the departments within that district. I live in an area that isn't very populous or prosperous, and many questions were asked about the amount of money the fire district was spending. A surprisingly large percentage of voters couldn't understand why it took so much money to keep our "little" fire stations operational. (To be fair, the fire officials weren't terribly good at explaining it to the voting public.)

The answer is simply that it's expensive to maintain equipment and personnel in a state of perpetual readiness. Our fire departments have medical personnel, firefighters, and an array of costly equipment for everything from house fires to car crashes to forest fires (we live on the edge of wilderness, and forest fires are a common threat). That's a lot of equipment to maintain, and a lot of people whose skills need regular practice if they're to stay proficient. Expecting all of that to work every time, on a moment's notice, requires resources.

Resources cost money.

Similarly, maintaining your family's readiness for a wide range of hazards is expensive. Remember, your preparedness resources include not just money but your time, interest, and energy as well. Those resources are what you have left over after you spend most of your week at work and after you pay the mortgage and heating bills for the month. As I've said before, they're limited!

The more skills you learn and the more equipment you acquire, the larger the drain on your resources to maintain them in a state of readiness. Lots of people make lots of preparations, some of them very elaborate, but find they don't have the time or inclination (let alone the money) to make sure they're actually usable over time. That's a mistake; it's better to focus on a few vital skills you can maintain inside of your preparedness resources budget than try to keep up with a huge assortment of gear and skills.

Back to my defensive shooting example: I've had many students who've taken many shooting classes, learning a huge range of techniques and concepts. A large percentage of them never get out and practice those skills, and as a result start from scratch in every new course they take. They'd be far better off if they'd stopped after the first course and simply maintained the skills they'd learned at a usable level. As it is, their lack of practice sometimes means they're little better prepared than the person who's had no training at all.

Over-preparation can be as risky as under-preparation. Use the information you've learned in this chapter to prepare appropriately, equip yourself rationally, and devote the necessary resources to practice your skills and maintain your gear over the long haul. That's how you become truly prepared!

Maintaining equipment

Maintenance also means making sure your gear works. You probably change your smoke alarm batteries on a regular schedule; you should do the equivalent with every other piece of safety/rescue gear you have.

Firearms

If you have defensive firearms, maintenance means keeping them reasonably clean and properly lubricated. If you shoot the gun a lot (and you should, to maintain your skills), follow the manufacturer's maintenance schedule. Springs wear out, parts fatigue, and sometimes things break. Replacing parts on schedule and lubricating the gun as recommended go a long way to ensuring the gun functions when you want it to.

Many people aren't aware, for instance, that the recoil and magazine springs on semiautomatic pistols have a finite life and should be replaced. Some guns have parts that are known to break or fail at specific intervals. Knowing this, and keeping those parts on hand, help guarantee reliability. Guns carried next to the body, particularly those carried in the pocket, are somewhat prone to rust. A regular maintenance routine will catch that before it becomes a problem.

Emergency kits and more

If you have medical kits, inspect them at least yearly. Many medical supplies have expiration dates, and while it's true those dates are exceedingly conservative and going past them rarely results in harm, it's still a good idea to replace anything that is significantly past expiration or whose packaging has been damaged. Hemostatic agents (which stop bleeding by encouraging clotting) have expiration dates, as do most drugs and antibiotic products.

If you have survival kits, such as the aforementioned "get home" or "bug out" bags, their contents should be checked in the same way you check your medical kits. Any emergency food you have stored should be examined and, if past its expiration date, replaced. (Most food expiration dates can be safely ignored. They're more guidelines for good taste and texture than for food safety. Still, who wants to eat crappy food in an emergency? Bad food is a serious detriment to morale, and in a disaster you want to do everything you can to maintain your spirits. Fresh food is a very good way to do that. If your emergency food is expired, eat it now and replace it with fresh. You'll be happier when it's the only thing you have to eat.) *

If you have spare clothing in your kits, periodically check that it still fits. Because of where we live, we have wildfire evacuation kits. I packed them some years ago and recently discovered, much to my chagrin, that I could no longer fit into the pants! That probably says more about me than about my emergency kit, but it's those little details that regular inspections are designed to catch.

Do you have an emergency generator? It needs to be tested at least yearly, and fuel and oil need to be changed on a regular basis — even if the generator isn't run. (Test your generator by putting in a small amount of gasoline, then running until it's out of fuel. This purges the fuel system and greatly reduces issues such as clogged carburetors. Never store fully fueled gasoline engines for long periods!)

I could go on, but I hope the point is made. Any physical item, be it gear, food, or medical supply, should be regularly checked and maintained. If you add it to your calendar and treat it like any other to-do in your life, it won't take up a lot of your time, but could mean the difference between success and failure when it's called upon.

Dedicated training and practice gear

If you practice your skills with the gear you have, your gear will experience wear. In many cases, it's prudent to have separate training gear that is a duplicate of the items you'll actually use.

The best example is your trauma response kit. Elsewhere I've suggested that everyone needs to understand how to deal with life-threatening trauma such as bleeding. To do so, you need a trauma kit, which typically consists of a tourniquet, some sort of hemostatic dressing (usually gauze or a sponge-like material), and a pressure bandage. It goes without saying that you can't reuse a bandage, and while no such restrictions apply to the tourniquet, they do experience significant wear when used — even in practice.

Having a dedicated training bandage and tourniquet with which you can regularly practice makes eminent sense. Tourniquet makers usually offer colored versions of their products to help differentiate practice and "live" versions for just this reason.

Of course, if you have a defensive firearm, you probably have different ammunition for training and carry/defense. Practicing your skills at the range or taking a defensive shooting class uses up a lot of ammunition. Quality defensive ammunition isn't cheap, so just about everyone practices with cheap full metal jacket ammo and saves the expensive hollow-points for carry and staging. But what about the gun itself?

If you can afford it, having an exact duplicate of your carry/defense gun may be a prudent expenditure. The training gun is the one you take to the range and to class and the one that gets all the wear. Your carry gun is shot enough to verify its reliability, then only carried (and maintained). This way, when parts inevitably break or wear out and cause the gun to be unreliable, it affects your training gun— not the one you rely on. This is an admittedly expensive proposition, but if you're serious about practicing your defensive shooting skills, I contend it's worth the expenditure.

You can no doubt think of other preparedness areas where dedicating a specific piece of gear to regular training and practice might be advisable. Look through your preparations and consider where you can benefit from doing so.

* — *I'm generally against maintaining a special stock of "emergency food." I prefer to keep a large stock of the food I normally eat, so that my diet doesn't change radically in an emergency. Not everyone agrees with me, hence the recommendation.*

OPTIMIZING OVER TIME

Every so often, I look back at my emergency planning from years ago and am amazed at how bad some of it was. I'm sure in ten years I'll look back at what I'm doing today and think the same thing! Over the several decades I've been doing this, I've continuously optimized my personal security plans. I've learned more, I've improved my skills, technology has changed dramatically, and expectations have risen. Some threats have become far less likely, while others have become more likely.

As a result of all those changes, my planning has evolved. As I've trained and practiced, I've made mistakes, corrected those mistakes, then retrained and practiced the changes. From big things to little details, I've gotten better — sometimes in leaps, other times in baby steps, but each time at bat (I hope), I've learned and grown.

Because you and your life are never static, your Adaptive Personal Security planning is never really finished. Your goal should be to optimize over time, taking advantage of the changes in your life and the world around you to become safer than you were yesterday.

Changes in circumstance

Everything that happens in your life is likely to change your security planning in some way. Your income might increase or decrease. Your career may give you more or less free time. You might move from the rural Midwest to an urban enclave on the East or West Coast. Your living quarters could change from an apartment in the city to a house in the suburbs, or from a condo to a farm. Perhaps you'll go from enjoying the single life to having a family and increased responsibilities. If you have a family, eventually your kids will grow up and move out, leaving you with a house full of empty rooms. You're going to age — I can guarantee, if nothing else, this *will* happen — and it will change everything.

Are the threats you identified then still the ones you face now? Some may have disappeared and others appeared. For instance, where I live in the Pacific Northwest, we have to be concerned about earthquakes. Were I to move to Indiana, I could probably forget about the earthquakes but would need to plan for tornadoes. Some of the plans would stay the same and some would change, but I wouldn't know which unless I reviewed my planning.

Has your financial situation changed? Your plans may have been compromised by the need to work within a budget, but could now be altered to a "best-case" solution because you can afford it. The opposite, of course, might occur as well.

As your children grow, their security needs change. When they were young, you had one set of worries, but now they're out driving and facing a new set of risks. Maybe you started your preparations when you were single, but now you have a wife and a child on the way. Such a happy event will definitely change your plans!

As each of these things changes, so too will the threats you face and your ability to Respond to a life-altering incident. As you work through your plans, ask yourself, "What has changed?" If you're lucky enough to have been able to put into place every piece of your Adaptive Personal Security plan, part of your maintenance routine should be to go back and re-evaluate your base assumptions.

Changes in technology

Technology is constantly changing. In fact, sometimes it changes so rapidly that things become obsolete overnight. This kind of change definitely impacts your planning.

Here's one example: just a few years ago, it was very expensive, and very difficult, to install any sort of video surveillance system (and all they did was continuously record poor-quality video.) Today, "smart" cameras are available that connect easily to your computer network and can recognize the difference between people and animals. They can be configured to record superbly detailed video only when something trips their recognition software. In the future, perhaps they'll incorporate facial recognition, which will give you a friendly chime when your familiar UPS driver puts a package on your porch, but an alarm when a stranger tries to steal that package.

I'm old enough to have been an early adopter of cell-phone technology. My first cell phone was known as a "bag phone." The phone was literally in a soft-sided case that was carried around by a shoulder strap. It had a handset connected by a cord to the phone itself. The whole package was the size of an old-fashioned lunchbox and weighed several pounds.

Today, I have a smartphone that contains more computing capability than the first five computers I owned — combined! It has tremendous capabilities, from reporting my position to monitoring the lighting in my home.

All this technology has applications for personal safety and family protection. It makes many parts of security planning easier, while bringing new risks itself. Keeping up on these technological changes is admittedly daunting, and I don't recommend becoming an early adopter or slave to the latest innovations. But I do recommend you evaluate the technology you're using to keep yourself safe every year or so, and take advantage of advances when they make sense for you.

Changes in society

It's easy to get sucked into the belief that the "old days" were somehow better than today. I can see why people might think so; days gone by seem more stable than they are now. Having lived past the age of 50 gives me a perspective I never expected to have, and I've come to the conclusion that, no matter how good the old days seem now, we certainly didn't think so when they were the "now" days!

What's undeniable, though, is society does change. It might not be as fast as we want, and sometimes it happens much too quickly, but change is constant. When I was just out of college, concealed carry was almost unheard of. People didn't routinely carry firearms, and if they did, they did so illegally. Aside from police officers, the only people generally assumed to be armed were bankers and jewelers.* Carrying a firearm just wasn't the norm.

In fact, the whole topic of self-defense with a firearm wasn't often talked about. When I look at gun magazines from the 1950s and 1960s, what sufficed for self-defense talk were somewhat fanciful articles on "combat shooting," and even those were a little on the fringe of the shooting community.

Today, "shall-issue" concealed carry is common in almost all states — with a few glaring exceptions — and the doctrine of the use of lethal force in self-defense is both well established and widely discussed. Entire classes and books are devoted to the practical and legal aspects of self-defense, and even people you wouldn't expect to be armed have concealed-carry licenses. If defensive shooting isn't mainstream, it's awfully close!

This carries through to preparedness in general. No longer is it generally seen as odd or concerning that people are taking responsibility for their own safety and security. (In a way it's something of a throwback to the first half of the twentieth century, when taking care of yourself was expected.) This means it's easier to plan for your own safety and the security of your family and loved ones. More products and sources of information are available than ever before, sometimes making for an embarrassment of riches. New products and services are introduced regularly, many of which have utility for your preparedness.

But keep in mind that public perception is a fickle beast. What society accepts today it may not tomorrow, and so maintaining a low profile is always a good idea. The more paranoid members of the preparedness community refer to this by the military acronym "OPSEC": OPerational SECurity. Don't broadcast what you do or what preparations you've made.

No one needs to know you carry a defensive handgun or that you've made arrangements for food and electricity during a disaster. What seems normal today could become abnormal tomorrow, and societies will generally seek out and punish the abnormal. Your focus should always be on taking care of yourself and your loved ones, but doing so quietly. Preparedness isn't about external validation!

Going back, making progress

When you have all the items in your Adaptive Personal Security matrix checked off, it doesn't necessarily mean you've done everything you can. There may be more you can do to increase your safety against your identified threats. For example, you may have hardened your doors and installed motion-sensing outdoor lighting to Deter burglars and home invaders and checked off that portion of your matrix. But you could still do more, assuming you have the necessary resources (time, energy, money, and interest) to do them. You could fence your yard and get a dog to help Deter intruders and serve as an early warning system. Maybe it's time for a video surveillance system or monitored alarm.

The point of the matrix is to make you safer one step at a time. If you just do all the things you put into the cells in your matrix, you're going to be safer than you were before. In fact, the reason I suggest this approach is because it's easy to make constant incremental progress. A little thing here, a little bigger thing there, and before you know it, you're far better off than you would have been if you hadn't done anything. If you do nothing else but what you've written down, you'll be much farther ahead than the vast majority of people.

It's perfectly okay to stop at that point, as long as you commit to maintaining the things you've done. Whether practicing skills or keeping up on rotation and repairs, preserving your investment over a long period of time is crucial to preserving your safety. At the same time, understand that by iterating — filling out another matrix, but with new and different actions — you'll increase your personal and family safety even more.

It's helpful to review those matrixes, especially the ones you've checked off, every so often. As you do so, ask yourself two questions:

1) Has anything changed in circumstance, technology, or society that affects what I've done (or planned to do)?

and

2) Can I do anything more to make my preparations against this threat even better?

You may find yourself altering your plans to reflect the new environment in which you live. You might need to replace something you've already done with something more suited to a new situation, or you might augment previous preparations with additional items that have a synergistic effect on your safety and security.

Reviewing your plans with an eye to making them better one step at a time pays dividends over the long haul. Adaptive Personal Security focuses your attention on the short-term accomplishments that provide long-term results.

---

* — And little old ladies. When I was growing up in the 1960s, my Dad told me to be polite to the old ladies in our community because "they usually have a gun in their purse." Only when I got older did I discover that to be true in a surprising number of cases! Such is the power of having the personal fortitude to ignore what society thinks of you and instead concentrate on ensuring your own safety. There is a lesson to be learned from their example.

Part Two

DETER

Deterrence is the term for all the things you do that keep danger and its consequences away from you — whether through physical or psychological means, or some combination of both. Deterrence is about putting into place structures and procedures designed to keep dangers from turning into proximate threats.

People usually think of Deterrence in terms of keeping bad guys out of their house using bars and fences. That's certainly a big part of Deterrence, but it's not the whole picture. What if the threat isn't a person — let's say it's a flood. Is there still such a thing as Deterrence? Refer back to the definition: keeping the threat away from you. Deterring a flood might mean sandbags: they keep the water away.

Deterrence is a huge part of Adaptive Personal Security and the area which is likely, for most of us, to result in the greatest risk reduction.

Active or passive?

Deterrence can be both active and passive. Active Deterrence refers to protective measures that work only when the threat is present, or that require some sort of input from you. Active Deterrents are the things you do, or the tools you use, on an ongoing basis to keep the threat from affecting you or your loved ones. A protective dog, for instance, doesn't need to be specially trained to scare off an intruder. Any dog that barks and snarls at strangers will serve as active security. When a potential attacker isn't present, the dogs' protective abilities aren't used, and they're simply happy companions. (In the case of my dogs, they're happy companions who eat a lot!)

Passive Deterrence, on the other hand, refers to things you put into place ahead of time and that work continuously, regardless of your own activity or the presence of a threat. Once in place, they work day and night, whether you're home to watch them or not. Locks on bicycles and your home's security doors are examples of passive Deterrents against theft and intrusion. Clear space around your home and fire-resistant roofing are examples of passive Deterrents against wildfire.

Overlap with other functions

As I mentioned in the section on Anticipation, some things can fall into more than one role. Sometimes Deterrents play more than one role in your personal security planning. The aforementioned dog serves as both an active Deterrent and a good early warning system. Visible security cameras might scare away many intruders and, at the same time, work as part of the Detect function to alert you to the location and intention of an intruder. Going even further, the recordings they make may be useful in the Recovery activities of the Respond function.

This again points out why the Adaptive Personal Security framework is so useful: It lets you see all the various parts so you can clearly understand where your strengths and weaknesses are!

LOWERING YOUR EXPOSURE

There is an old Japanese saying: "The nail that sticks up gets hammered down." Your first step in Deter is to strive not to be that nail! If you're exposed to the threat, you are more likely to suffer damage when that threat appears. If you can reduce your exposure — not be the nail that's sticking up — you can dramatically reduce your chances of becoming a victim of that threat, or at least reduce the damage the threat can visit upon you.

This is a difficult chapter to write, and for some it's going to be a difficult chapter to read. If your plan is to keep the threat from affecting your life and the lives of your loved ones, sometimes it means making attitude and lifestyle changes. I know changing your life isn't the most pleasant thing to contemplate. After all, you shouldn't need to. You should be able to do whatever you want as long as you don't infringe on the rights of others, and you should be able to expect the same in return.

Unfortunately, the world doesn't work like that. The nail that sticks up is a target, an impediment, something to catch things that come by. It's a dangerous position in which to be when trouble comes knocking.

Personal crimes

Here's a question for you: How much do you know about muggings — the crime of attacking and robbing someone in a public place? What do muggers look for, and how do they pick their victims?

NBC in New York decided to find out*, and what they learned didn't surprise any of us who study these things: Muggers look for targets who look lucrative and appear easy to overcome. The largest percentage of the criminals NBC contacted said they were looking for "nice" clothing and jewelry, worn by someone who looks like they wouldn't fight back. Most of the criminals carried weapons, and in suburban settings preferred to attack victims in their driveways.

Similar surveys have been done with burglars and other criminals, and the results are absolutely clear: If you look like a valuable target, and especially if you look easy to overpower, you're far more likely to be targeted. "Random" crimes are seldom all that random. Criminals pick and choose their victims, and the less you look like one, the less likely you are to become one.

Avoiding the criminal

Let's start with the obvious: If you wear expensive clothes and jewelry, drive an expensive car, and generally look like an affluent person, you will attract more unwanted criminal attention than the person who doesn't flaunt their wealth.

This is especially true in areas where displays of wealth are uncommon. If you dress "to the nines" ** in Manhattan, you're probably going to look like a lot of other people. You might not get a second glance unless you're famous. On the other hand, if you dress like that in, say, Detroit, you're likely to attract unwanted attention from the wrong sort of people.

The first step in lowering your victim profile is to not look out of place relative to the environment. We all want to show off a little, to display our success and good taste, but that isn't always appropriate — let alone safe. Take heed of what other people look (and act) like and strive to imitate them.

Don't look like a victim

It's one thing to not look like a lucrative resource, but it's another to not look like a victim. If you appear to be an easy mark, you're more likely to be targeted than someone who looks like they'd put up a fight. This is critical for non-theft attacks: who doesn't appear to be aware of their surroundings or who doesn't appear to have the ability to defend themselves, is more likely to be singled out for attack.

Your first step is to not look like someone who'd be an easy mark. When out in public, keep your nose out of your smartphone! Wait until you have more control over your immediate surroundings and can monitor who's taking notice of your activities before checking your phone. Walk confidently, with your head up and eyes looking around.

Start thinking of distractions as criminal bait. Savvy predators look for openings in your armor — times and circumstances where they can attack with the least risk and highest chance for success. Don't give them those openings! Manage your distractions and avoid looking like you're not aware of what's going on around you.

Don't look like a tourist

This is important if you travel to foreign countries. Tourists are a favorite target of criminals and scammers, and Americans in particular are ripe targets all across the globe. We're seen as rich and naive, and while the former may not be true, the latter almost always is! If you're traveling, study up before your departure. Learn the customs and common dress of the people where you're going. (It wouldn't hurt to learn a little about their language as well.)

When I was growing up, the stereotypical giveaway for an American tourist was Bermuda shorts combined with loud shirts. Today, it's the ubiquitous baseball cap. We don't think anything of them, but they're not common in most other parts of the world (and even where they are, they're never worn backward in the bad-boy style so common in this country). The simple act of wearing a ball cap instantly signals "tourist" and serves as a beacon for criminals in the area. An easy way to reduce your exposure is to leave the baseball cap at home.

It should go without saying that conspicuous displays of wealth are always dangerous. Electronic goods, including cameras, are prized theft targets in many parts of the world — especially those where the locals can't afford such luxuries.

Property crimes

A property crime is one in which your possessions are taken, but you're not personally targeted (or even present). It's easy to think of all crimes as being personal, and to a certain extent they are, but property crimes are thefts and burglaries of your house, car, or business when you're not present or not expected to be present.

Like personal crimes, lowering your property crime risk is a matter of making your home and property less inviting to thieves. Making sure your blinds are closed when you're not home, not leaving expensive property like bicycles out in the open, and keeping your plants and trees trimmed so burglars don't have a place to hide are all part of lowering your exposure.

In many ways, the idea here is to make your property less inviting than that of your neighbors. This always seems a little harsh when I say it, a bit like forcing the toxic waste dump out of your community and into the one across the tracks. But the reality is, unless he's put in prison, the burglar is going to ply his trade somewhere. Make sure he doesn't do so at your house.

Like not flaunting personal wealth in the form of expensive jewelry, reducing your property crime risk means keeping your possessions to yourself. If the burglar doesn't know you have it, he's less likely to try to steal it.

Don't make it easy for him

Another avenue for Deterring property crime is to make sure you're not helping the thief. If you've left out in your yard tools the burglar can use to break in, you've made his job easier. If you've hardened your ground-floor entrances but left a ladder out to reach the unprotected upstairs windows, you've essentially given him an invitation.

Look at your property with an eye toward improvised tools. Have you left a moderately resourceful thief things that he could use to batter down your back door? To break through a basement window? Don't give him any help!

Social violence

Criminal encounters can be roughly split into two categories: asocial violence, also known as resource predation, where the criminal expects to get something from you; and social violence, where the incident happens as a result of intimidation, disrespect, or turf-guarding.

A good example of social violence is the classic bar fight. People get a little drunk, insults escalate, and before you know it, fists (and sometimes knives or guns) are flying. No one expects to gain anything other than saving their face or pride. A road-rage incident is similar: One driver does something another finds offensive, rude words and gestures are exchanged, and before you know it, two people are brawling on the side of the road.

Social violence often starts with ritualized posturing. If you're in an unfamiliar environment, one in which the culture of interaction is different than the environment you're accustomed to, the specifics of the posturing may be misconstrued. In those cases, conflict may be inevitable.

Lowering your risk for social violence is really a matter, as famed self-defense trainer John Farnam is fond of saying, of not doing stupid things in stupid places with stupid people. If you can avoid doing those things, you've dramatically lowered your risk of a social violence incident.

Learning to put aside your ego and say "I'm sorry" is also a good way to lower your risk profile. The person who has to save face, to show he's as much of a man as the next guy, is the type who often finds himself at the wrong end of a broken beer bottle. Swallowing your pride greatly reduces the chance that someone will take you up on your macho challenge.

Avoiding social violence means paying attention to what you're doing and what you're saying. If you can just do that, you'll greatly lower your exposure — and you'll have a better time, too!

Disasters

Can you lower your exposure to natural disasters? After all, "acts of God" are generally held to be outside of our control (hence the attribution to a supreme being). If you can't control them, how are you going to lower your exposure?

You can start by carefully choosing where you want to live. Some places in every area are safer from certain incidents than other places. If you live in a region prone to floods, you can choose to live on higher ground. (The same is true for tsunamis.)

If you can't avoid the danger, such as in hurricane or earthquake country, you can choose to live in a home that's more resistant to those disasters. Is wildfire a concern? Pick a home that has large defensible spaces and fire-resistant siding and roofing.

You can't avoid everything, but you can substantially reduce your risk by making some careful choices.

Health

As I mentioned in an earlier chapter, your own health is by and large within your control. Of course you can't do much about your genetics, but even if your ancestors weren't completely disease free, you can still choose a healthier lifestyle for yourself.

Lowering your exposure might mean making dietary changes or eliminating unhealthy habits. It might mean committing to regular checkups and screenings, or perhaps an exercise regimen. Whatever it is, think of your health just like any other aspect of your preparedness, and start by lowering your exposure to health-related dangers.

*—

www.nj.com/news/index.ssf/2017/02/muggers_dont_discriminate_on_who_they_rob_report_s.html

** — *A positively out-of-date expression meaning to dress elaborately or in the finest fashion.*

*** — *More in the chapter on Becoming a Harder Target*

CHANGING THE RISK/REWARD EQUATION

If the threat you're preparing for is a human one, a key component of Deterrence is changing his (or her) risk/reward calculation.

The term "criminal activity" covers a wide range of incidents. Burglaries, robberies, carjackings, muggings, sexual assaults, and more fall into this category. Even personal crimes have disparate motivations: Social violence covers things that happen without a goal or reward, such as road rage, while asocial violence deals with crimes that involve seeking a reward — tangible or intangible.

I won't go into a deep discussion of all the kinds of crime to which you might be vulnerable. Entire books have been written on various aspects of criminal activity, and I encourage you to avail yourself of them. In this chapter, I focus on how to use Deterrence to avoid interacting with a criminal in the first place.

How humans make decisions

You and I make risk/reward calculations all the time. In fact, this book is all about those calculations. Whether consciously or subconsciously, we evaluate the things we choose to do and if the reward doesn't exceed the risk, we're less likely to do the action.

For instance, I know of a mountain bike trail complex featuring all kinds of ramps, jumps, and other riding challenges. I've watched the riders and to me it looks like a whole lot of fun. I'd love to try it myself, but there's one little hitch: I'm not much of a mountain biker. I don't have their equipment or stamina, nor does my aging body possess their recuperative powers. Were I to take a spill from one of the elevated trestles, I'd probably die. Or if I didn't, I'd probably wish I had!

Because of the risk involved, I'm not going to make the mistake of trying it myself. The reward wouldn't be worth the almost certain injuries I'd receive. It's a basic calculation based on my knowledge of my own limitations (and of what a broken bone feels like). You make these same kinds of assessments every day.

Criminals too, whether they know it or not and whether they'd understand it or not, are very likely to do the same thing. They weigh what they'll get from their victim and decide if the risk of capture or injury is worth it. They're not walking around with spreadsheets on laptops, but they make these decisions nonetheless — because that's what humans do.

The criminal might take his time to observe traffic patterns and habits before burglarizing your home (many do), or he might make a quick on-the-fly decision to target a specific person on the street. Whether deliberate or hasty, his analysis will determine if he risks his freedom on you. It's also important to remember that any drugs in his system may affect his perception of either the risk or the reward. His calculation may not make sense to you, but it will to him — at least until he sobers up.

When we're talking about criminal activity, changing his risk/reward calculation in your favor is one of the keys to keeping him away from you.

Disrupting the expert

The predator is likely to make use of his knowledge of the street and of the behaviors of victims. In this area he's the expert, and like any expert in any field, the more experience he has under his belt, the less he needs to think about what he's doing. He makes decisions based on what he knows, on the patterns he's observed with other victims. He might not even be doing his assessment consciously, because as he gains more experience, he needs to rely less and less on such cognitive analysis. He knows what a victim, a lucrative target, looks and acts like and makes his decisions based on past experience.

The less you look like what he already knows to be a profitable opportunity, the more likely he is to stay away from you. There are two ways to do this: make it appear as though little reward is available, or make it appear that a high degree of risk is associated with the reward.

Decreasing the reward

As we saw in the chapter on lowering your exposure, convincing the predator there is nothing to be gained from an attack on either you or your property is a low-cost, high-yield defensive strategy. The classic example is not wearing flashy jewelry while walking down the street in a dangerous part of town. It would seem to be a common-sense approach to living, but I find a surprising amount of resistance to the idea!

Let's get this out of the way immediately, because it will hamper your ability to keep yourself safe in many situations: Yes, you have the "right" to go and do whatever you want. You shouldn't "need to" worry about how your behavior appears to criminals. None of that matters, because along with all the other things they don't respect, criminals don't care what you have the "right" to do.

While I don't like it myself, the reality is you need to consider what kind of target you present to others around you. Conspicuous displays of wealth may in fact attract burglars and muggers. If you choose to show off what you have, you also have to accept that it will raise your victim profile. At the risk of repeating myself, whether that's "right" or "fair" doesn't enter into the equation. It's simply the way our world works. As someone told me many years ago, that's reality — you can either use it to your advantage or it will automatically work against you.

What might you do to reduce your victim profile? As already noted, avoiding conspicuous displays of wealth is certainly one way. Not frequenting high crime areas is another. Not driving in urban stop-and-go traffic with your windows rolled down (or the convertible top down) might keep you from looking like a prime carjacking target. Avoiding window decals, both auto and home, that suggest you have valuable items present, keeps the potential criminal from knowing his time will be well rewarded. If a criminal sees you favor high-dollar brands of easily fenced merchandise (especially firearms), it gives him a piece of information that tips his risk/reward calculation.

Around the home, not leaving expensive bicycles on the porch or having easily accessible burglary tools (such as ladders) lying around change the risk/reward calculation in your favor. Keeping window blinds shut when you're not around, making it harder for a burglar to window shop, is another way to change his decision.

Another tactic is to deny the criminal the kind of vital information he needs to make his decision. In tactical circles, this is often referred to as "OPSEC," or operational security: giving out information only on a need-to-know basis. Everything you do that's visible to the public gives onlookers information about you, and while most people generally ignore those signs, you're not concerned with most people. You're concerned with certain people who look for that information and use it to choose their target.

Deny them that information. Be careful what you do, what you show, and what you say.

Increasing the risk

The other side of the risk/reward calculation is convincing your potential attacker what he might get from you isn't worth the potential jail time or injury he might suffer in the process.

Countless research projects and experiments have shown that humans are more motivated to avoid pain than to seek gain. Increasing the apparent risk of an attack against you or your property suggests to the criminal he's more likely to experience pain than to achieve any gain.

If the criminal is under the influence of drugs or alcohol, however, his impairment may cause him to misjudge either the pain or the gain. People's judgements are less reliable when their brains are chemically impaired. In extreme cases, even the infliction of actual pain isn't enough to Deter them. This illustrates a vital aspect of preparedness that most people want to ignore: Sometimes you can do everything "right" and still lose.

Humans are also motivated to take the path of least resistance. In a very real sense, it's not necessary to present an absolute level of risk to the criminal. As long as you appear to be a greater risk to him than the person next to you, the criminal is very likely to target the other guy instead. There's an old joke (stop me if you've heard it) about two hikers confronted by a grizzly bear. One starts to run, while the other calmly takes off his hiking boots and puts on running shoes. "Are you crazy?"his friend exclaims. "You can't outrun a bear!"

The reply was, "I don't need to outrun the bear. I only need to outrun you!"

I must admit a bit of shame when I put it in those terms. After all, I'd rather see a criminal dealt with and spend time behind bars than "passing the buck" and sending him across the street to some other victim. But the reality is, you're unlikely to catch a criminal without substantial risk to yourself. Even if you did, our justice system is so crowded that only the most heinous criminals will see serious jail time. The best thing you can do for your own protection is to ensure he doesn't choose you as his next victim. Rest assured, no matter how you or I feel, he's going to pick someone — your job is to make sure he doesn't pick you!

All criminals are not equal

Not every criminal is equally motivated, equally determined, or equally skilled. Like all other areas of human endeavor, there is some sort of "bell curve" of criminal ability. Not every predator you encounter is like every other one. You might run across one who's deterred by a strong stare, while the next one may not be swayed by anything less than gunfire. Some will bypass alarms and locks easily, while another will choose a different target if he sees an alarm company decal in your window.

As in any other field of human activity, the more highly skilled/more motivated/more determined criminals are rarer than the lesser-skilled ones. They may be fewer in number, but they're the most dangerous. No matter how many layers of security you erect between you and everyone else, someone will be capable of breaking through them. Ultimately you need the ability to protect yourself should you come face-to-face with that person — the "worst-case" scenario.

Some violence isn't about risk/reward

An important point is that social violence, those incidents caused by a clash of personalities or cultures, is rarely diffused by a show of force or by an analysis of risk and reward. In fact, a show of force may be seen as a challenge which demands a response. It's very difficult to dissuade social violence through an increase in displayed risk. It's much better handled by de-escalation and a refusal to be dragged into a primitive contest of strength.

BECOMING A HARDER TARGET

A big part of keeping the threat and its consequences away from you is doing things that ward off the threat. As I've mentioned, it's normal to think of Deterrence in terms of measures like burglar-resistant bars across the windows. That's one common method to protect against property crimes, and it falls under the general category of "target hardening."

In its simplest terms, target hardening means to strengthen security in order to protect from attack. For our purposes, the meaning of target hardening is expanded to encompass anything you do to keep a threat from affecting you, your loved ones, or your property.

There may be some overlap between hardening and lowering your exposure, particularly when talking about crime. On occasion you may identify something you do to reduce your victim profile that will also make it harder for the criminal to reach you, and vice-versa. That's a happy efficiency!

In most cases, though, the hardening you do simply serves the purpose of keeping the threat from directly affecting you. Hardening is a vital part of preparedness, and for each threat you face, you should think about what you can do to keep it from reaching you or others in your family.

Property crime

There are two components to hardening your property. The first is to physically prevent someone from breaking into and stealing your property. Security doors, bars on the windows, good locks, and reinforced door frames are perfect examples: They make it physically difficult for a criminal to do his job, and many a burglar has been turned away simply by locked doors.

Sounds stupidly simple, but you'd be surprised how many people don't lock their houses or cars. Greg Ellifritz, a police officer in Ohio, reports on his blog* that some 70% of the home and vehicle thefts he investigates occur because the victim didn't take the simple expedient of locking their doors!

The second component is convincing the bad guy your property isn't worth the risk or effort. If you can convince him your property isn't as attractive as others in the neighborhood, he'll usually take the easiest route and go somewhere else.

Deterrents like motion-sensing floodlights that come on when someone strays into their sensor range are a good way to do that. Thieves don't like light. It calls attention to them and what they're doing. Of course they're only effective at night, while a large portion of residential thefts occur in broad daylight. Making bad guys think twice while you're at work can often be done by a large dog, which burglars overwhelmingly say they avoid day or night.

Make them work for it

Making sure you have good deadbolts on solid doors, and reinforcing the door frames into which they lock, is a way of keeping bad guys out of your house. One of the characteristics of burglars is that they want to be in and out as quickly as possible, and the longer it takes them to get in, the less they're likely to persist. If they know there's a big reward inside (because you didn't heed the advice about keeping valuables out of easy view), they might persist. But if they're not sure, they will likely move on to an easier target. The same thing can be said for windows and glass doors.

Alarm systems are another Deterrent. If the prospective thief knows there's an alarm present, again without the assurance of a payoff, he's likely to look for an easier target. Some burglars report passing houses up merely because of an alarm system sign in the yard.

Making the burglar believe your house isn't worth the effort, that's it's going to take a lot of time or energy or risk to access, and then physically denying him access is a hardening recipe for lowering your property crime risk.

Some of these Deterrents are also part of the Detect function we'll cover in the next chapter. Hardening can mean visible alarm or video systems and large dogs, which are also great tools to alert you to the presence of danger. I call these "dual duty" preparations, which are a very efficient use of your preparedness resources. Whenever you can get dual duty out of a preparedness activity, give it a little higher priority in your planning.

Personal crime

How do you personally present a harder target?

Learning self-defense skills tends to have the effect of changing how you carry yourself. As it happens, you don't necessarily need to learn self-defense or carry a defensive firearm (though both may be a good idea) to take advantage of this. Paying attention to the messages you give off with your posture and gait, and changing them to appear more self-confident, tell potential attackers you're not an easy target.

Managing your distractions, such as not allowing yourself to be sucked into the screen of your smartphone, sets you apart from the crowd. Keeping your head up and your eyes moving suggests to a potential attacker that you're not going to make it easy for them. While certainly not foolproof, it does suggest to the bad guy that he might want to look for someone who's easier to victimize because they're not paying attention to what's going on around them and/or because they look meek or fearful.

Walking purposefully, not allowing yourself to be weighed down with bags or packages, and staying physically fit are all ways to project a capable, prepared image to those around you. That's the kind of person criminals tend to avoid. As someone once said, "If you look like food, you will be eaten!"** Not looking like food is the first step in hardening against personal crime.

Information security

In today's world, information security is an important part of target hardening.

One downside of the internet age is a lack of online privacy. Like it or not, you can learn a lot about others — including details you might be surprised to see — online. If you can do it, so can others. It's a big concern for everyone because such information can be used to target you when you're most vulnerable. The savvy criminal can use available information to figure out if you'll be a profitable target, what your weaknesses are, when you're easiest to attack (or when your house is likely to be unoccupied), when your children are vulnerable, and more. This information can also be used to perpetrate electronic and financial crimes.

Start your data hardening process by clamping down on the personal information trail you leave online. Your social media profiles should never have personally identifying information such as your birthday or your mother's maiden name (the latter is often provided when people share pictures of their family history). Obfuscate any useful information such as where you used to live, where you live now, your phone number, your children's names, and anything else that might be used by someone pretending to be you.

Make sure your tablets and smartphones are locked when not in use, and use passcodes that are more than four characters long. If your device has it, turn on the "destruct all information" option, which erases the device if there are a certain number of unsuccessful access attempts.

A great source for information security and protecting your data is the Your Ultimate Security Guide blog, which deals with a wide range of information security and privacy issues in a straightforward and readable way: www.blog.yourultimatesecurity.guide

* — *www.activeresponsetraining.net/lock-your-damn-doors-2017-edition*

** — *Variously attributed to either John Farnam or Clint Smith.*

DETERRENCE BEYOND CRIME

Up to this point, we've been looking at Deterrence from the stand-point of crime: how to keep criminals and their activities away from you and your family. But Deterrence goes beyond bad guys, and it's useful to think about what you can do to keep other kinds of threats from impacting you and your life.

A good example is one I live with myself: Deterring wildfire. I live in the woods, and I'm surrounded by hundreds of thousands of acres of unoccupied forest. Fires in this area are a fact of life during the dry season. So dire is the threat that all work and travel in the forest are prohibited at the peak of summer. Around here, we take the risk of wildfire quite seriously.

At my house, we Deter the spread of wildfire by establishing defensible zones around the house and outbuildings: clear areas that will hopefully slow or even stop an encroaching fire. These zones are specifically intended to Deter fire by making it harder for the fire to progress. Like any Deterrent, they may not be perfectly effective (and I hope to never find out), but it's one thing in our wildfire arsenal to reduce its impact.

Of course we have Response plans in place should the fire "jump the lines," and we have evacuation kits if we're forced to leave on short notice, but the Deterrents in place will hopefully prevent going that far. Such is the job of Deterrents.

Think about other threats you face in your life. Are there any you can physically prevent from harming you? A shelter in tornado country can be thought of as both a Deter and a Respond tool. In earthquake country, seismic retrofitting is a kind of Deterrent against building collapse.

As you fill out your threat matrixes, it's useful to ask yourself if you can put something in place to keep the threat away, some barrier you can impose that will physically separate you from the threat. Can something insulate you from the effects of the threat? Those are all Deterrents. Think about what damage the threat does, how that damage is accomplished, and then think of ways to prevent that damage from affecting you and your life.

That's the essence of all Deterrence.

Part Three

DETECT

Detect covers things that alert you to an unfolding threat. Detect ranges from the passive, such as alarms, to the active, such as your understanding and use of situational awareness. In all cases, Detect exists to give you advance notice. It gives you time to Respond. The more time you have, the more options you'll be able to choose from.

But Detect isn't just for immediate threats. It also gives you the opportunity to identify possible threats well enough ahead of time to plan and prepare for them. In a way, this whole book can be said to be about Detection! Becoming aware of a danger to your life or well-being and making plans to mitigate the threat are made possible by a good Detect strategy.

A caution goes along with this chapter: Don't let any Detect plans, no matter how elaborate or extensive, blind you to the need to be able to Respond to an immediate threat. It's tempting to think you're so prepared nothing could possibly hurt you, but the reality is you won't see everything. It's entirely possible for human predators to get past your Deter and Detect plans and surprise you. You still must prepare to deal with the threat you didn't see coming ahead of time, to implement a credible Response even if you're caught off guard.

This is especially important when talking about personal self-defense. Many people have been brought up with the idea that their superior "situational awareness" will keep them from ever needing to fight back against an attacker. It's just not true, and the worst part is the threat that makes it past your Deterrence and Detection is likely to be the most dangerous.

Detecting the threat is important, and in fact critical to your total personal security. But understand that it's never perfect. Strive to make it better all the time, while understanding it's never finished and never infallible. You don't have to be paranoid, but you must acknowledge that, even with diligent preparation, you can still be surprised. Hope for the best, but plan for the worst.

EARLY WARNING SYSTEMS

A key component of Detect is early warning: getting advance notice of a threat. That's what makes Detection so valuable. Learning about the threat as far before it appears as possible allows you to prepare an effective response. The more time you have to Respond, the less you need to improvise in the heat of the moment — and the more likely your Response is to be successful.

Alarm systems

I'll bet your first thought when you saw the title "early warning systems" was "alarm." That's a normal first thought, because the alarm is the perfect example of an early warning system. It alerts you to the presence of someone whose intent is, at best, unclear.

You might be thinking, "The alarm only works when the bad guy actually breaks in. How much of a warning is that?" More than you'd have if you woke up with the bad guy standing at the foot of your bed! No, it's not a lot of time, but in reality — and assuming you've thought about how you'd Respond to a midnight break-in — it's enough to put your practiced Response plan into action.

The worst-case scenario is to be caught off-guard by an intruder. The closer the threat is to you, the more difficult it is to defend yourself. If, on the other hand, your alarm went off because he broke a window, you'd likely have enough advance notice to lock your bedroom door, retrieve your defensive firearm, and call the police to alert them that someone is in your house.

Those seconds of early warning might mean the difference between the police capturing your intruder without any risk to you, or you fighting it out in close quarters with someone dangerous. Never underestimate the advantage of a head start!

Not just for burglars

It should go without saying, but alarm systems can also be multi-hazard warning devices. Smoke detectors save lives every year by warning sleeping occupants of fire. If you use a fireplace or woodstove for heat, a carbon-monoxide detector is just as important (and many are combined with smoke detectors for another kind of multi-hazard protection). The advance notice they give you may be the difference between a close call and being found lifeless in your bed.

Some of the newer "smart" alarms even incorporate severe weather alerts, such as tornado warnings, into their systems. If you live in tornado country, you understand the value of early warning in the event of a destructive twister, and having that warning as part of a total security package increases your preparedness — especially when you're asleep.

Animals

Don't overlook low-tech early warning systems in your plans! Animals, particularly dogs, are a time-honored alert system (as well as being good active Deterrents). A loyal dog barks at perceived danger both day and night, and is sensitive to potential threats that even the best alarm system won't detect. I am always amazed at what a dog can sense long before I see or hear it.

A dog doesn't need to be specially trained for this function. While you can get specialized guard dogs who are trained to attack a threat, they're both expensive and difficult to handle on a daily basis. Any loyal dog will bark when a stranger shows up, which is really all you need him (or her) to do. A good dog can give you plenty of time to decide how to handle a developing incident.

Size isn't important, either. Even the smallest dogs bark their heads off in the presence of a stranger, and in fact the smaller the dog, the more vocal they seem to be about such things!

In the Deterrence section, I pointed out that a dog is a good multi-role defensive asset. In addition to the early warning advantage, dogs also scare off a lot of people — criminals included. Again, your dog doesn't need to be trained to do this. It's a natural reaction to anything that threatens the pack.

Don't expect an untrained animal to fight off an attacker, though. Without special conditioning, it's rare to find a dog that will maintain a protective posture when seriously threatened or struck by an attacker. Lots of people believe their untrained Golden Retriever is "so loyal it will fight off anyone who attacks my wife or children," but nothing could be further from the truth. Most dogs run as soon as someone hits them hard enough.

Dogs are great protective tools, and I believe one should be a part of most people's personal security planning if at all possible, but it's dangerous to over-estimate their abilities. If you want a true protective dog, one that will fight an attacker against all resistance, you need to seek one out and pay considerable money. You also need training yourself in how to handle him.

Other animals have been suggested as good early warning systems. Many people tout geese as protective animals, and there is some basis for the recommendation. Just a few geese will certainly alert you to the presence of anyone who shouldn't be there. Geese are territorial and very vocal when anything intrudes on their environment. They're also quite aggressive and will savagely attack interlopers, be they human or animal. But unlike dogs, they can't be trained NOT to alert or attack, and that trait means you have to put up with a lot of false alarms. In short: They're noisy, and they're never not noisy! Proceed with caution, and of course only if you live on acreage.

Surveillance systems

Many modern alarm systems combine alert features with surveillance features, but they can also be installed and configured separately.

Surveillance systems do two jobs: They give you information about where intruders are, how many there are, and what they're doing; and they collect and store that information as evidence so you have something concrete to give to law enforcement.

Modern surveillance systems go well beyond those functions, which is why they overlap with alarm systems. Newer cameras are capable of monitoring an area for movement, turning on their recording only when they sense movement. This detection can be infrared or optical, or a combination of both. Some newer cameras have fuzzy logic systems built in, which allows them to distinguish between the movement of an animal and that of a human being.

These cameras are often wireless or sometimes hardwired (ethernet) into your computer system. Combined with software on the computer, they can set off an alarm to alert you of an intruder, track his movement among cameras, and even let you hear and speak. Facial recognition software is rapidly increasing in capability and dropping in price, and by the time you read this, it may be commonly available as camera firmware.

The changing technology means these systems no longer require you to hire a security company to put them together. While they're not quite plug-and-play, they're getting very close and require only a small amount of technical know-how to install and operate. All the necessary pieces can be purchased online from mainstream sites like Amazon, and they're surprisingly affordable for the technology they contain. Long gone are the days when only the rich could afford them.

Modern surveillance systems are so easy to install and so affordable that there's no longer an excuse not to have one in your home.

(One caution: Be sure to learn about securing those video cameras from outside access. With internet-connected cameras, it's possible for a hacker to view or even control them, allowing a potential attacker to gain valuable intelligence about you and your activities. Have strong passwords on the cameras and on the software that controls them.)

Intelligence gathering

This may seem an odd entry in Detect, but knowing the kinds of threats you face and the form they take is a big part of being able to recognize them when they appear. Intelligence gathering, or learning about those threats and how they manifest themselves, is an important tool for Responding appropriately.

You've already learned about the need for information security, but one of the pluses to the river of data we call the internet is the wide availability of information on the threats you might face. With just a few keystrokes, you can pull up all kinds of data about your town and even your neighborhood: what kinds of crimes happen, where they happen, and how often they happen. You can even monitor potential predators in your area, as most police departments have maps or locations of registered sex offenders.

Knowing these things helps you decide how and what to prepare. If you know, for instance, that nighttime burglaries of occupied dwellings occur more often than daytime intrusions when no one is home, it would suggest more emphasis on early detection systems and family defense. If a large number of assaults happen on the jogging trails in a wooded parkland, it would suggest moving your workout runs to a local high school track.

Be careful interpreting crime statistics

A few years ago, I attended a large convention in a medium-sized city. The number of visitors was large enough to overwhelm all the hotels within a 30-mile radius of the city. Two other people attended with me. We decided to rent a house through a popular online service.

The description of the neighborhood was "an eclectic artist community." The area had lots of greenery and gardens, and two churches were on the block. Everything looked good, but since this wasn't a hotel with security, I did my due diligence and checked crime reports for the area. I found the quadrant of the city where the neighborhood was located had a higher crime rate than the rest of the city, but this neighborhood and the adjoining one enjoyed less crime. I decided it was a good choice and booked the house.

Imagine my surprise when we arrived and the police officer who was part of our group witnessed a drug deal happening on the corner! He judged the neighborhood to be, in his exact words, "sketchy at best." The house across the street looked like it was straight out of a dystopian movie set. How could this be, when my research indicated this location had a lower crime rate than the city as a whole?

As my cop friend explained, statistics are made up of *reported* crimes. In some instances, people can become so inured to crime that they stop reporting any but the very worst incidents. When you have a lot of crime in one neighborhood, the residents start to fend for themselves, and as a result the reported crime rate can go down even when the incidence is actually quite high. In his estimation, that's what was going on in this neighborhood.

Let's just say I didn't sleep well for the four days we were there!

Statistics are a great indicator of what might be happening, but they're not the whole story. If you see abnormally low crime statistics where you live or work, ask questions: Is it because crime really is lower there, or are other factors skewing the results?

You might be surprised at how this happens. Another police officer of my acquaintance told me of a small scandal in his city. It was home to a well-known university, and a large amount of political power was centered in the school. According to him, this political clout was used over many years to pressure the city to under-report crimes in the area where the school was located. This had been common knowledge to the residents for decades, but out-of-state students (and their families) were led to believe the area was safer than it really was. Newcomers to the neighborhoods around the university were often surprised to find out that home-invasion robberies and sexual assaults occurred at a much higher rate than even the less-affluent areas.

Don't let apparently positive crime statistics lead you to believe your neighborhood is "safe." It's true that crime rates aren't uniform anywhere, and there are areas where crime is better than others — and areas where it's much worse. Don't let your guard down, or be convinced not to prepare at all, just because the data looks good.

What's better than knowing your neighbors?

Often overlooked in this impersonal day and age is the simple expedient of getting to know your neighbors. Aside from learning about current events, good neighbors can be called upon if you need help — in return they can call on you if they need assistance. To use an old phrase, "That's what neighbors are for."

If you have retired neighbors, be especially sure to cultivate their friendship. They're often home when you're working and, because they have time to talk to other people, they get the scuttlebutt about what's going on in the area. Gossip may be a sin in some people's eyes, but it can be an important source of intelligence for you!

Retirees have probably cultivated relationships with other people in the area who have eyes and ears "on the ground." You should also get to know these people if at all possible: the mail carriers, parcel company employees, trash collectors, and others who are in your neighborhood on at least a weekly, if not daily, basis.

You'd be surprised what your letter carrier knows. She gets around, talks to people, sees what kind of mail they're getting, and generally hears all kinds of comments you might not. The same goes for parcel delivery people. More than once I've been amazed at what I've heard from ours — information that has almost always proven to be accurate. I'll bet yours can do the same.

Even the local utility company technicians can give you vital intelligence. They often work their assigned geographical areas for years and get to know the pulse of the neighborhoods. They know who's coming and going, and very often why.

In short, talk to people. Be friendly, ask questions, and listen. Anyone who spends time in your neighborhood, whether it's where you live or where you work, knows something. Ask them what they know, and whenever you hear something interesting, ask yourself, "How can I use this knowledge to increase my personal security?"

Properly used, intelligence can be the ultimate early warning system. It just needs a little attention from you and the willingness to make new friends!

SITUATIONAL AWARENESS

A big part of Detection is recognizing a developing threat before it becomes dangerous. In the self-defense world, this is often referred to as "situational awareness": the ability to see and predict things based on environmental cues.

Unfortunately the concept of situational awareness is often both misunderstood and oversold. It's touted as a magical state of being where you can see everything before it happens, thus keeping you in a bubble and safe from harm. Many people seem to believe their superior situational awareness negates the need for any other skills. The reality is that situational awareness isn't magic, and it's not foolproof. It's simply another part of your self-defense and personal security skillsets; a very important part, but not the only part.

I'm not a fan of the term "situational awareness," because it implies a universality that isn't accurate. It also suggests focusing on everything without a thought as to what is important and what isn't. I much prefer the term "threat awareness," which is a far better descriptor of the skill you need to develop. It's the term I'll use throughout this chapter and the rest of the book.

What is threat awareness?

Threat awareness is nothing more than using your knowledge and skill to recognize, avoid, and (if necessary) act on threats to your physical safety. It is your personal early-warning system. Like an alarm for your home, a well-honed threat awareness gives you time to decide and implement a course of action before the threat can harm you. That early warning may only be seconds, but that's enough to make the difference in the outcome of a violent incident.

Threat awareness is a marvelous skill to develop, because it helps you see the difference between real threats and the innocuous everyday activities of normal people. In an ironic twist, I've found that developing good threat awareness has the benefit of making me more aware of life around me. Because it enables me to focus my attention on what's important, it's efficient — which frees up a portion of my limited attention to allow me to appreciate the little things in life.

Remember what I said in the beginning about seeking peace? A well-honed sense of threat awareness is, I believe, almost a necessity to achieving that.

This chapter only scratches the surface of the concept. A thorough discussion would take an entire book. But in brief, starting to develop your own threat awareness comes down to four simple steps:

1) Minimize your self-imposed distractions

2) Learn to recognize attack precursors

3) Develop an avoidance paradigm

4) Develop a counter-ambush approach to defense

Let's look at each of these.

Minimize your own distractions

I put this first on the list because it's the most important to the threat awareness process. You only have so much attention; you cannot manufacture additional attention on demand. Your brain, and its sensory inputs, have only so much bandwidth available. It's not a matter of multitasking (which is a fallacy), but rather task-slicing. Your brain can switch attention from one task to another, but that requires you to want to switch attention. The term distraction, as I use it here, means the monopolization of your attention by a single activity.

Sometimes monopolization is a good thing. When you're attacked, for instance, all your brain's activity is taken up in dealing with that threat. The threat monopolizes your attention and you're fixated on defeating it. That's your natural threat reaction in a nutshell; it's normal and necessary.

It's the unnecessary (and usually voluntary) task fixation — distraction — that you need to avoid, at least when you're in an unsecured or uncontrolled environment.

Look at the people around you, at work or on the street. How many of them are preoccupied with themselves and their activities? The primary source of distraction today has to be the ubiquitous smartphone. Whether checking for text messages or updating Instagram, people everywhere seem to have their faces buried in the devices. On the street, in the restaurant, and even while shopping, the smartphone occupies an inordinate amount of human attention.

It's the most common distraction, but it's certainly not the only one. Reading a book, uninterrupted window shopping, or simple daydreaming all use up valuable awareness that may be better used to look for patterns that might signal impending criminal activity.

Being conscious of your own distractions is the biggest step you can take in minimizing them. Do you really need to use all your awareness on one task, or can you efficiently task-switch? How about saving non-urgent tasks for a time when you can better control your environment (i.e., in your office or at home)? At the very least, put away that smartphone when you're on the street!

Recognize the signs of an attack

Learning how criminals attack is an important part of recognition. Once you understand that criminals target their victims, even if very briefly, you can spot their rudimentary surveillance ahead of time. Knowing how criminals "interview" their victims, or how criminals working in pairs flank their targets, allows you to evade or counter their attempts.

When dealing with social violence, those attacks in which ego and pride are the motivators, studying pre-assault indicators is an important part of learning to de-escalate an impending attack. Watching for the telltale unconscious signs that people give off may give you precious time to avoid being punched. So important is this field of study that police officers spend a good portion of their training time learning exactly what those signs are and how to defuse a situation before force is needed.

Some time spent studying how mass-casualty attacks happen may help you spot emerging incidents and pre-emptively evade the area. Knowing how bombs are usually placed, and understanding the behavior of the people who place them, may give you the time you need to alert authorities so the area can be cleared.

Little substitute exists for knowing how attackers behave and achieve their goals. Your recognition of the attack before it happens gives you survival options. The information is available, but you need to seek it out as part of your planning and education.

Think avoidance

Any defensive incident you're involved in is likely to have life-altering effects, even if you're completely successful in defending yourself. Shooting another human being, especially if he dies from his wounds, will change your life forever — and if the defenders I've talked with are any indication, likely not for the better.

Knowing an attack may be in the offing gives you options for avoiding the situation altogether, which is by far the best defense you can have. Recognizing the precursors of an attack gives you the time you need to formulate an avoidance option. Your well-honed skill in quickly and systematically looking for the signs of an impending attack will also alert you to avenues of escape you may not have noticed, and the occasional thought of "What would I do *if...?*" will help you develop that avoidance ability.

You can't avoid that which you don't know is happening. Threat awareness is all about figuring out what might happen and then working out a way to make it not happen to you.

Prepare for the ambush

One of the notions other progressive defensive trainers and I reject is that somehow you can maintain such a high level of awareness that you'll always see everything coming. The reality of threat awareness is that you won't see everything. You simply can't. Acknowledging this is a huge step forward in your defensive mindset.

No matter how good your awareness, it's always possible for someone to slip under your radar and surprise you. Whether because of a well-honed attack skillset or sheer dumb luck, someone will eventually pierce your awareness shield and surprise — ambush — you. This is the attack you need to be ready for, because it's the most difficult to defend against.

A counter-ambush approach means developing defensive skills that work when you're caught off guard and haven't had any chance to formulate even a brief Response. Counter-ambush is reactionary defense in its purest form: You're reacting to a situation you didn't see coming until it was right in front of you.

The reason I mention this as a separate item, and an important one, is because the skills and techniques you use when you've been surprised are useful even when you have some advance warning of an attack. The converse isn't always true; skills that work when you know you're going to need to fight won't necessarily work when you have no warning of an incoming attack. The counter-ambush mindset is an important part of being able to Respond to a wide range of attacks.*

If your defensive skills require you to get into just the right position or use just the right tools, or ignore the physical changes in your mind and body that occur as the result of a surprise lethal attack, they are not by definition counter-ambush skills. You need skills that work when you're off balance, when you don't have time to get into a perfect stance, and when your vision and attention are fixated on your threat. Counter-ambush skills take into account physiological changes in posture, tactile sensitivity, and vision.

If that doesn't describe your self-defense skills, seek out training that does if you expect to have good counter-ambush ability.

Hyper-vigilance isn't the answer

Many people talk about "situational awareness" in terms of color codes or other shorthand. Their contention is that if you live in some sort of hyper-vigilant state, you'll be safer because you'll always see the attack coming in time to prepare for it. (This notion is also used to disparage the idea of counter-ambush skills, because if you're always alert, you can't be ambushed!)

The reality is simple: You can't live a life of hyper-vigilance. Your brain on't allow it for prolonged periods of time without significant physical and psychological effects. In practice, it's impractical to achieve because you have more things to do during the day besides guard duty! Using your attention to be aware of everything in your environment is very inefficient, because most of what's in the environment has no relationship to any potential threat.

It's common for proponents of hyper-vigilance to have students do memory tests. They look at a scene and memorize some arbitrary and unimportant sequence or look for and count something like license plates. These exercises purport to develop "situational awareness" through hyper-vigilance, but all they really do is train people to waste their brain's clock cycles on irrelevancies.

Even if those exercises somehow worked, even if you could maintain this mythical state of hyper-vigilance without side effects, someone would still occasionally slip under your radar and surprise you. If that surprise happens to be in the form of a criminal, your lack of understanding of the counter-ambush defensive posture might leave you woefully unprepared to deal with the threat.

Forget hyper-vigilance. Focus instead on eliminating your distractions, recognizing what's important in your environment, figuring out ahead of time how you'll avoid a threat, and have the skills in place to deal with those that get through.

* — *Counter-Ambush online course:*

www.personaldefensenetwork.com/class/counter-ambush-concepts-preparing-your-response/

Part Four

RESPOND

Respond is really a phase of activity. It's what you do when your Deterrence and Detection haven't been able to prevent danger from reaching you. Respond is what you do when a threat — be it human or Mother Nature — manifests itself. Respond is what you do "in the moment" to protect your life and well-being and those of the people around you. Respond is focused on the incident itself as it happens.

The message in this book so far has been to do everything you can to keep the threat away from you so you aren't forced to Respond. Unfortunately you can't prevent or forestall everything. No matter how well you Deter a threat or how early you Detect it, sometimes that won't be enough. In those instances, you'll be forced to Respond.

When that happens, you're likely to be caught off-balance. I'd love to tell you that your perfect Detection planning will always and without fail give you plenty of advance notice, but that's not the way the world works! No matter how prepared and aware you are, some threats will make it through your security and protection layers. In those times, you're forced to deal with the threat as it is, not how you wish it would be.

Any Response that doesn't take that into account, whether in self-defense or disaster survival, isn't realistic. Your Response planning, equipment, and training all need to be predicated on the idea that you didn't see the threat coming and now need to protect yourself in the face of death.

You might be thinking, "If those other things don't always work, why bother with them? Why not just do all my planning for Response?" Good question! Because the closer you get to a threat, the closer you get to a Response, the more danger you're in. Not everyone survives a Response, even if it's successful. Deterrence is a far better survival strategy than confrontation. Early Detection allows you to possibly avoid the threat, or if you must face it head-on, at least gives you extra time to formulate a less risky Response.

Deter and Detect work a very large portion of the time. I'm not saying they're not valuable, only that your planning needs to take into account those times when they won't be enough. It's about optimizing your Response to work over the greatest range of variables.

You won't find a lot of specifics in this section, because each topic could warrant a book of its own. Instead, I'll show you what you should consider in your Response *planning* — the things you should know and study more in depth. This isn't about what you should do, but what you should prepare to do!

Response is the sexy part of self-defense

One reason I wrote this book is because of the defensive training world's over-emphasis on Response. Studying martial arts or learning how to shoot well are two common Response-level activities. They're fun and exciting. They're sexy! It's fun to get out and shoot guns or throw people on the ground. If you haven't tried either, you probably won't believe me, but it's true.

As I've said in many of my other works, those skills don't actually keep you safe in the sense of preventing a threat from impacting your life. By the time you need to Respond, the threat has already impacted you — you're just trying to survive the impact.

Response skills give you the ability to rescue yourself when the threat has appeared. They are ways of escaping an already bad situation. Safety, on the other hand, means not getting into the bad situation in the first place. Hence, Deter and Detect.

The trouble is that Deter and Detect aren't fun, and they certainly aren't all that sexy. They're just unexciting work that pays big dividends. The result is an over-emphasis on Respond operations in the Anticipate planning stage.

Because Respond is so alluring, it's easy to spend an inordinate amount of your preparedness resources on it. Many people in the defensive shooting world get so wrapped up in "developing their shooting skills" that they neglect other areas of their personal security preparations. Shooting is expensive: Shooting classes cost a lot of time and money, not counting the ongoing practice to maintain those skills. You'd be surprised how many defensive shooting hobbyists have no early warning systems or even know how to deal with life-threatening trauma, which is an everyday occurrence no matter where you live.

Deep or wide?

Ask yourself if your Response preparations are better handled by going wide or deep. Again using defensive shooting as an example, many people take shooting courses of ever-increasing difficulty. Are those "advanced" courses necessary for self-defense against any plausible predators? I've never found a case where they were. Going deep in a specialized Response skill such as defensive shooting may not result in an increased likelihood of survival against plausible threats, but it will result in increased expenditure of time, money, and energy.

Focus your efforts and preparedness resources on safety — avoiding the threat — but have Response skills and plans in place for when you can't avoid the threat. Don't let the tail wag the dog!

Keeping on track

It's possible to get so wrapped up in your Response preparations that you run out of attention and forget about what will keep you from needing to use those skills. One of the key benefits of the Adaptive Personal Security approach, and of the matrix, is they allow you to track what you're doing for each threat and see where you need to allocate your limited preparation resources.

Watch for an overallocation of resources when you fill out your matrixes. Compare what you plan to spend on Response versus Deterrence and Detection. If you use the matrix conscientiously, you'll automatically put the proper amount of resources into each function of your self-protection. It's hard to forget to do something when it's sitting right under your nose!

Responses aren't always universal

In the beginning, I mentioned there is a lot of overlap in the things you do for the Deter and Detect functions. The plans you make to deal with one potential threat are often effective or useful against other threats as well.

As you get into Respond phase, this becomes less true. The personal defensive firearm, for instance, is the ultimate example of a special purpose tool. It's useful only against a very narrow range of threats in a very narrow range of circumstances. In fact, the gun is probably the most specialized personal security tool you're likely to own. It just so happens that when you've fallen into the specific circumstances that call for a specialized tool, it's the most efficient way to rescue yourself!

You can see it in the contents of this section. The Respond functions take up more space, and are more specific, because they tend to be a little more specific to the threat. When you're doing your planning in the Anticipate stage, you'll probably see this in action.

This phase consumes so many resources due to the specialized nature of Response tools and skills. In accounting terms, you can't usually apportion the costs of Response knowledge and equipment over as many threats. If you're preparing specialized Responses for a huge number of threats, you'll spend your resources rapidly. This is why the exercise of identifying plausible threats (which you learned in the beginning of the book) is so vital: It keeps you from spending your limited resources in areas that aren't really important.

The importance of recovery

Part of Respond is recovering from the ordeal. We don't talk about Recovery much in the world of self-defense and preparedness, because it's not exciting or sexy. It doesn't involve heroics or cool gear. But it's necessary, because the point of Adaptive Personal Security isn't only to protect your life — it's to enable you to continue living that life. Recovery is vital to rebuilding your life after a critical incident.

When we think of Recovery, we think of activities like rebuilding after a flood or hurricane, but that's just scratching the surface. Recovery from a criminal attack, for instance, might involve legal representation to navigate the criminal justice system. Even though you might not face criminal charges for defending yourself, you may be faced with a civil suit from the criminal (or his family).

Recovery of all kinds may involve psychological counseling, but particularly so if your self-defense Response resulted in the loss of your attacker's life.

Even in natural disasters, though, psychological scars remain. The mother of a good friend worked with the American Red Cross for decades, going to disaster sites and counseling the survivors whose entire lives had been disrupted. (This underscores the value of being prepared ahead of time. As she explained, the people who were ready for the disaster often helped others cope with what had happened.) She related that victims of severe disasters often had ongoing and long-lived emotional issues that required professional help. Understand you might need such help, and factor it into your Recovery planning.

SELF-DEFENSE

You may be reading this because of an interest in self-defense. In fact, many of us came to the study of personal security through the sub-topic of self-defense. It's a core component of all preparedness, and it could be said that preparedness is nothing more than self-defense against the widest possible set of threats.

But in this book, we're going to limit the term "self-defense" to dealing with a criminal attack against your person. This is the image most people have of the term, and we'll explore other aspects of the broader definition later. Self-defense is the perfect example of the Respond function: Everything you've done to keep the threat from reaching you has failed, and you need to take action to survive the incident as it unfolds.

The Response of self-defense is initiated when you're faced with a criminal predator. He may be attracted to you as a victim because he wants something tangible from you (resource predator), because he wants to exert power over you, or because you failed to avoid an inter-personal incident that resulted in social violence.

But at the point you need to defend yourself, his motivation ceases to matter, because now you need to keep him from hurting or killing you.

The danger of self-defense

If you've worked on your Deterrence and Detection against a criminal predator, you've put into place measures to keep the criminal from getting close to you. Whether it's because you've installed barriers to physically keep him away from you, changed his risk/reward decisions, or simply reduced your criminal "radar signature," you've hopefully done something to prevent becoming a victim.

You should also have done something to Detect his approach. Perhaps you've worked on your observation and prediction skills, or maybe you've put in some sort of early warning system to alert you to his presence. Whatever it is, being forewarned is a huge step toward avoiding the situation altogether.

But the reality of the human predator is that he may be sufficiently motivated and crafty enough to make it past your Deter and Detect preparations. The person who does is very dangerous, because he's proven he has both the dedication and the skill to get to you. He will also likely have surprised you with his sudden appearance and caught you off guard.

Any self-defense program you embark on needs to be predicated on the idea that you've been surprised by your attacker. First, because it's the likely situation. Second, because the self-defense skills that work when you're surprised are going to work equally well when you have some advance notice, but the opposite isn't likely to be true. If your self-defense preparations are based on the idea that you'll always know ahead of time when you'll be attacked, you'll be caught off balance by the attack you failed to see coming.

Should you check off the Deter and Detect functions in your matrixes before working on the Respond aspects of self-defense? Only you can answer that, based on your own accounting of the actual threats you face. Keep in mind, though, that Deterrence and Detection help address many kinds of threats; self-defense, only one.

Self-defense options

When talking about a self-defense Response, we're talking about the use of countervailing force — force that causes your attacker to stop what he's doing. Since your attacker is a human being, and human beings vary greatly in their psychological and I physical makeup, the force required may range from minimal to lethal.

Martial arts

The various martial arts are valuable when your attacker is in contact with you. They can't be used, except perhaps as a threat, at any distance much beyond arm's reach. They all require you to be touching your attacker — the most dangerous position to be in.

At the same time, a large number of surprise attacks are initiated when the predator grabs his victim. Physical contact may be your indication that an attack is happening, and knowing how to counteract such an attack may be your best option.

What are the issues with relying on martial arts as your primary or whole Response? First, they take time to learn. Most of the well-known martial arts are very formalized and ritualistic, requiring (and expecting) the student to dedicate himself or herself to long study to become proficient. They also have strong components of self-actualization and spiritual development, which are not directly applicable to your goal of learning to stop an attack.

Some traditional martial arts have evolved into purely competitive activities, and this competition base means what they teach may not always be directly applicable to self-defense in the real world. Any system that requires compliance on the part of the training partner to function as taught probably won't work against a non-compliant attacker.

Martial arts also require a certain amount of physical strength. As you age, a martial arts Response becomes less usable, and injuries can reduce your effectiveness substantially. Many martial arts rely less on strength than on leverage, but they all demand some strength and flexibility. Because of their physicality, injuries during training are a very real possibility (and almost inevitable in some styles). Again, as you age and your ability to recover from injuries decreases, studying a martial art becomes less attractive.

I'm not an expert on martial arts in any sense, but I've come to the conclusion after some study that their best use is in facilitating your escape. Forget flying kicks to disable multiple attackers, like you see Jackie Chan doing. What you really want to learn is how to get away from an attacker, or at least get beyond contact range. For that, Brazilian Jiu-Jitsu (BJJ) is probably the best choice. It's based on using technique and leverage against a larger attacker, and has a strong emphasis on grappling and fighting on the ground. Ensure that your BJJ instructor is focused on self-defense as opposed solely to competition. The same goes for all martial arts.

Be wary of "systems" purportedly originating from military special forces that promise fast results with little study. Many are on the market, and they often combine unrealistic scenarios with techniques better suited to fit young men.

Less-Than-Lethal tools

In the world of self-defense, invasive tools like the gun and knife are considered lethal force: Shooting or stabbing someone is likely to kill them outright unless they receive immediate medical attention. Tools that are not invasive but designed to inflict pain and discomfort without significant damage to the body, are called "Less-Than-Lethal" (often abbreviated LTL).

LTL tools include impact weapons (batons, canes), chemical sprays (pepper spray, MACE), electrical devices ("stun" guns, TASERs), and control tools (Kubotans and other pressure-point tools, high-intensity flashlights). LTL tools can also serve multiple roles: A high-intensity flashlight can be used as a pressure-point tool and an impact weapon.

Think of Less-Than-Lethal tools as intermediate-force weapons.

They're useful when dealing with a threat that presents a non-life-threatening injury potential. The firearm is a specialized tool applicable only to a very small percentage of incidents. The LTL tool is applicable over a wider range of interpersonal conflicts. Everyone who carries a defensive firearm should also have an LTL alternative, because not every incident rises to the level of lethal force. If your only tool or skill is shooting, you're ill-prepared for the many more common incidents where shooting isn't a viable Response.

The LTL tool may also be a credible defense against a lethal threat. The TASER shoots small barbs into an attacker and immobilizes him by sending electrical pulses that disrupt the function of large muscle groups. If someone attacks you with a knife, a TASER may drop him to the ground and allow you to escape unharmed. In many instances, people have used chemical sprays to effect the same result.

However, LTL tools have major downsides. First, all of them have significant failure rates. Chemical sprays are frequently ineffective against drugged or drunk assailants. Those who are inured to the effects of the pain-causing compounds, such as people who eat lots of very spicy foods, are also often not affected by sprays. If someone has already experienced a chemical spray, they likely know how to fight through its effects to continue their attack.

Even the much-vaunted TASER has a failure rate. Sometimes their barbs don't penetrate heavy clothing, or one of them misses the target, or they land too close together. Those will all render the electrical pulses partially or totally ineffective. Individuals who have been repeatedly "tased" may also have learned how to defeat the pulses by quickly ripping the barbs out of their skin.

Devices such as the stun gun are almost completely ineffective the majority of the time. In fact, they are so ineffective I believe it's borderline criminal to sell them as personal-defense tools!

A second downside is many of them require you to be in contact with the threat, which is where you're most vulnerable. Any control device, such as the Kubotan, as well as impact weapons, require you to be within arm's reach of your assailant. They can be useful if you're already in contact, but they don't allow you to keep an attacker from getting his hands on you in the first place.

Another issue (and this goes for all defensive tools, lethal or not) is they have a learning curve requiring training and practice. The Kubotan requires training and practice to use properly. Impact weapons also require some practice to employ to their fullest capability. Even seemingly easy tools, like the chemical sprays, benefit greatly from a short course in their use.

LTL tools are an important part of a total self-defense plan, but they're not magic wands. You should always have access to one, but understand its limitations before you rely on it as your sole means of self-defense.

Improvised weapons

If you're in an area where you can't carry effective weapons of any kind, you may be forced to press other objects into service. Improvised weapons refer to things that are part of your environment and that you use as tools to deflect an attacker, but that were not originally designed to do that job. A kitchen knife isn't an improvised weapon because you'll be using it to do the job for which it was designed: cutting and stabbing. A broken bottle does approximately the same thing, but was never intended to be used in that manner, hence it qualifies as an improvised weapon.

Making effective use of improvised weapons comes down to two things: being able to see the possibilities, and having the skill to use them to their potential.

Seeing the weapon potential in everyday objects is something of an acquired skill. We're not socially adapted to consider the ways in which we can hurt other people, and as a result, most students have a great deal of difficulty seeing the weapon potential of the items around them. But learning to do so is simply a matter of getting accustomed to looking at things with an eye toward how they can be used to hit, stab, slash, or disrupt the vision or breathing of an attacker. There are many books on the subject, and doing a web image search for improvised weapons will open your eyes to the possibilities.

The second part relates to the skill required to use them efficiently. If you don't know how to use a knife or baton effectively, you're not going to use a broken bottle or rolling pin as well as you could. Developing even a passing acquaintance with powerful stabbing, slashing, and hitting movements will greatly increase your potential with an improvised weapon.

Here's an exercise for you: Next time you're sitting in a boring meeting at work, look around the room and think about how you could use each object in it as a weapon against an attacker. Think about the wounding mechanism (impact, cutting, etc) and the physical manipulations necessary to make them work. This simple thought process will help you see the possibilities in your environment, no matter where you might find yourself. (And it will save you the embarrassment of falling asleep during the meeting!)

You can apply the same exercise to many areas of your life. For instance, if you're waiting for your significant other while shopping, or standing in line at the bank, you can look at your environment and see what objects you could use to defend yourself against an attacker.

Lethal weapons

When you're attacked by someone who intends to do you harm that could result in your death or permanent disability, we refer to that as a lethal threat. Lethal threats are, in virtually every jurisdiction, allowed to be met with lethal force in response.* When we talk about lethal force, we're generally talking about a firearm — although it also includes the defensive use of a knife.

Lethal force is generally seen as justifiable when the attacker poses an immediate and otherwise unavoidable danger of death or grave bodily harm to you or another innocent person. It is generally not seen as justifiable when you're merely scared. Your fear must be specific and it must be articulable. In other words, you must be able to clearly identify what posed a credible risk to your life and why lethal force was the reasonable Response. Jurisdictions vary on just what constitutes reasonable use of lethal force, and their interpretations may vary from case to case. It's important that you clearly understand when you can and can't use lethal force where you live and travel.

The gun

As I've said, the gun is a special-purpose tool for a very narrow range of events. It is the most efficient method of delivering lethal force to stop an attacker, and is usable at distances beyond arm's reach. It is, in fact, the only tool most people have that can be used more than a few steps away. The defensive firearm, be it a concealed handgun or a pre-staged rifle, requires training to be used to its fullest. While many people each year successfully defend themselves without training, others fail — either because they lack the shooting skills necessary to hit their target, or because they don't know when lethal force is and is not justified.

If you seek training in defensive shooting, don't get caught up in sales hype. The police and military use firearms very differently than you or I will, and it's best to find instructors who specialize in the use of lethal force by private citizens. Many ex-military and retired police officers go into firearms training without understanding the differences between their job and their students' needs, and as a result a lot of inappropriate training is being offered. Make sure your instructor understands what he or she is teaching and who they're teaching. **

The knife

The knife can also be an effective tool when lethal force is appropriate, but it suffers from two limitations: First, it's a contact weapon. Like Less-Than-Lethal contact weapons, to use a knife you must already be in the most dangerous type of situation: when your attacker has his hands on you. There may be some Deterrent effect to showing the knife and your willingness to use it, but to actually employ it, you're going to be touching.

The second issue with the knife is that it's very skill dependent. In other words, you need proper training and regular practice to utilize it effectively. More than just about any other defensive tool, the knife requires technique and skill to use. The knife is the lethal-force tool of choice for times when you can't carry a gun, but you need good training to use it effectively.

Concealed carry

Believe it or not, it wasn't that long ago when concealed handgun permits were hard to get and consequently rare. That started to change in the early 1980s, when the wave of "shall issue" concealed carry swept the nation. Today, the vast majority of states are required by their own laws to issue a concealed handgun permit to anyone who meets the statutory requirements. There are still a few holdouts — California, Hawaii, New York, Massachusetts, and Maryland are the most notable*** — but in the rest of the country, getting a permit to carry a concealed handgun is easy.

Having a defensive handgun always with you brings a certain peace of mind. The ability to defend yourself from a lethal threat no matter where you are extends your safety zone from around your house to around you, and by extension the people in your immediate care.

With rights always come responsibilities, and the concealed handgun brings with it a new set of concerns. You need to be very careful about when and how you use your gun. It's tempting to use it in situations where the use or threat of lethal force isn't warranted. In your home, the judgement is a little easier because you have a relatively controlled environment. Out in public, you need to practice avoidance more than at home.

You also need to carefully consider whether you'd come to the aid of someone in danger. We call this "intervention," and it's easy to find news stories of armed Good Samaritans coming to the aid of someone under attack. Unfortunately, you can also find many news stories of raging vigilantes inserting themselves into situations where their help was neither needed nor wanted. The difference in those two interpretations is whether the outcome was positive or negative!

Carrying a concealed handgun requires you to have control over your emotions, a clear understanding of the laws related both to carry and the use of lethal force, and a commitment to avoiding conflict if at all possible.

If you choose to carry a defensive firearm, you absolutely must learn the legalities of the use of lethal force. In fact, that should be the very first class you take.

Protection of property

Regardless of any local statute that suggests otherwise, the responsible person uses lethal force only when their life (or the lives of innocents) hangs in the balance. In a few jurisdictions in the United States, lethal force is technically allowed in the protection of property, but even in those areas, those laws are being rapidly modified by the courts.

Without getting into a sticky discussion about the morality and ethics of shooting someone, from a strictly practical point of view, it's not always a good tradeoff. Using lethal force against a burglar who has not posed an immediate threat to your life, particularly if he dies, will cost you and your family dearly. You may be arrested and forced to post bond. Even if that doesn't happen, you'll likely need to retain a lawyer to see you through the legal process. Depending on how good your lawyer is, that might cost you upwards of $50,000. If the prosecutor or grand jury decides that your case warrants a trial, you'll need to cough up around $100,000 almost immediately. If you win the criminal proceedings, you may still face a civil trial from the burglar's family. There's another $100,000 with the very real risk of a large award you'll be paying for the rest of your life.

It's not just the monetary damages, either. You'll discover, as many others already have, that your friends are likely to abandon you. No one wants to hang around with a "killer." Your children may find themselves ostracized both in school and out, and it's entirely possible you'll find yourself out of a job. Prospective employers avoid hiring someone with a "controversial" past.

Don't think it'll happen to you? Don't bet on it. I know people who have experienced all of the above. One person intervened in a fight using his lawfully carried firearm, didn't fire a shot, but found out — even two years after the fact — employers were reticent to hire him because of the incident. Imagine how much worse it would have been if he'd pulled the trigger!

Now, considering all I've said — and I've only scratched the surface — is that $350 television really worth it?

I see these scenarios play out constantly, all around the country. I've reviewed cases of teenagers getting shot while running away from a simple car prowl (break-in), and I've learned of innocent neighbors killed by bullets from the gun of the guy chasing the aforementioned teenagers. Lethal force isn't to be used as a control tool, it's not to be used to frighten people, and it's not to be used to stop petty crimes. Lethal force should only be used to protect your life from an immediate and articulable threat.

"I need a bigger form!"

You may find yourself putting several different types of Response options into your threat matrixes. For instance, a less-than-lethal option should always accompany a lethal-force option in your planning. If you find yourself running out of room for the options you want to implement, stop and think about your planning. Are you allocating so much to Respond in your planning because it's necessary, or because it's more fun? Is it because you really need training in several different kinds of firearms, or is it because you're a gun guy (or gun gal)?

Allow the matrix to do its job and help you efficiently allocate your scarce resources.

* — *This is not legal advice, and you are strongly urged to learn about the complex legalities that surround the use of lethal force in self-defense. The two best sources for this information are attorney Andrew Branca's superb book The Law of Self Defense, and Massad Ayoob's highly recommended course "Armed Citizen's Rules of Engagement."*

** — *"The two questions your defensive shooting instructor should be willing and able to answer":* www.grantcunningham.com/2014/02/the-two-questions-your-defensive-shooting-instructor-should-be-willing-and-able-to-answer/

and: "More questions you should ask your defensive shooting instructor — and why": www.grantcunningham.com/2015/08/more-questions-you-should-ask-your-defensive-shooting-instructor-and-why/

*** — *Some states that don't have a shall-issue law still allow individual counties to issue concealed handgun permits at their discretion. The criteria for those permits varies widely, and may have extremely limited provisions for when and where you can carry.*

HOME AND FAMILY DEFENSE

When I speak of home defense, I mean "defending yourself and your family while you're in your home or on your property." But that's a lot harder to say, so those of us in the defensive training world usually default to simply "home defense"!

I tell you this because it's very easy to think of home defense in terms of property rather than the people in and on that property. Hardly a week goes by when I don't hear of another case where an overzealous homeowner has shot someone for a mere property crime. While I have no love of the criminal element and in no way want to appear as though I'm defending their actions, I think it's important to point out that killing someone over a television is abhorrent. It may also land you in jail.

Instead I encourage you to focus on how to protect and defend your life and the lives of your loved ones. Some pre-planning will help, but first you need to grasp the basic principles. Understand that these are not an order of activity, but rather some things you might do to keep yourself safe.

Evade

If you can get away from the intruder, it's in your best interest to do so — but only if you can do it safely! Getting away from the bad guy and waiting for law enforcement to deal with him are preferable to facing him.

I realize some people might see this as cowardice, but it's really a pragmatic decision. Any confrontation, no matter how thoroughly you've stacked the deck in your favor, has the potential for your death or severe injury. The chances of you being hurt or killed by the bad guy are always greater than zero, and it doesn't matter how strong you are or how well you can shoot. You can reduce those chances to zero (or as close as you're likely to come) by simply not being there.

This might mean getting out of the house and to a neighbor's where you can call for help, but it can also mean just getting out of the intruder's immediate area. If the bad guy is coming in the kitchen window, running up the stairs to the second floor is a form of evasion. Think in terms of getting away from an area where the intruder has the advantage and to an area where you control the environment. In the case of the second floor, most houses only have one stairway, and it's an easy corridor to control. If you're at the top of the stairs and armed, it's very difficult for anyone to get to you. You are in the position of advantage, and you can defend it.

Evasion is the smart Response, but again only if you can do so safely!

Barricade

To barricade yourself means to shelter in an area where you can control access and make it harder for the intruder to physically harm you. A classic example of a barricaded position is the safe room: the room you've prepared ahead of time where you can be safe from an attacker.

A typical safe room is hardened so the bad guy can't easily break in, and prepared or "staged" with a defensive firearm and a way to call for help (a cell phone on a charger). Some people wisely include a trauma kit in the safe room to treat any family member who is injured.

Planning ahead and constructing a defensible barricade space may be a good use of your preparedness resources, but it's not the only approach to barricading. Any place you can get to where you can a) keep the bad guy physically separated and b) defend should he break through your defenses is a barricade.

If you choose to prepare a dedicated safe space, think first about how to gather your family in the space. If you don't have children at home, your safe space should probably be the master bedroom. It's where you spend about one-third of every 24 hours (and during a time when you're more vulnerable to attack) and thus is the most logical place (for most people).

If you have children, think about the need to gather them and bring them to the safe room. It's common for the master and secondary bedrooms to be on opposite sides of the house, or on opposite ends of a hallway with the entrance in the middle. In gathering the family, will you expose them to an uncleared or unsecured area during the trip? Will you expose yourself to those areas twice during the trip? If the answer to either is "yes," you might consider making one of your children's rooms the safe space.

Whichever room you choose, the door should be upgraded to a solid-core exterior type with a locking knob and reinforced jamb to resist a kick-in. If the room is on the second floor, it should have a retracting fire-escape ladder (all second-floor rooms really should, but especially the safe room!).

Arm

Arming yourself with weapons to fight the attacker is an important step in a home-defense Response. Naturally your first thoughts probably go to firearms: Retrieving your defensive firearm, be it a handgun, rifle, or shotgun, is something you should practice on a regular basis.

If you don't have a firearm, can't get to your firearm, or have a family member who can't or won't use the firearm, you can still arm yourself. What you use may not be as efficient as a defensive firearm, but that doesn't mean it can't be effective!

Think about household items that can be used to stab, slice, bludgeon, or disorient your attacker. Kitchen knives, hatchets, and machetes come immediately to mind as stabbing and slicing weapons. Baseball bats and golf clubs can be pressed into service as bludgeons. A fire extinguisher, sprayed in the attacker's face, can disorient by making it difficult to see and breathe — then the shell can be used as an impact weapon.

How about that fireplace poker? Depending on how it's made, it might be a stabbing and impact weapon. Look around the room -- what else might fit into those categories? Don't let the absence of a gun affect your thinking, and don't let what you can't do interfere with what you can do!

Communicate

In this case communicate means two things. First, communicating with the authorities to get help on the way. Having a phone with you, one whose wires can't be cut, and with which you can call 9-1-1, needs to be part of your barricade planning. If you don't have it pre-staged, it has to be on your person. Think ahead! Those old cell phones we all have lying around are perfect for the job, as by law even unactivated phones must be allowed to access the 9-1-1 system. Take your old cell phone, plug it into the charger, and put it in your safe space.

Communication may also mean with the bad guy. This is situational, but once you've barricaded and armed yourself (and have the police coming), you may choose to communicate to your intruder: "I'm armed and the police are on their way! Get out now!" If the bad guy knows you're there and where you are, there's no harm in letting him know you're prepared to defend yourself and that his best course of action is to leave.

If he doesn't know where you are, if you barricaded without him knowing you were even there, communicating your position isn't likely to be to your advantage. In such a case, quietly holding your position and waiting for the authorities to arrive, ready to respond if necessary, may be the best choice.

Fight

If all else fails -- if you were unable to evade or barricade or if the intruder has broken through your defenses -- you may have no choice but to fight.

Remember your job in fighting is to stop your attacker using whatever means are at your disposal. Someone who breaks through a barricaded position has likely demonstrated his willingness to hurt or kill innocent people, and you are likely to be justified in using lethal force to protect yourself and the other innocents in your home.

Understand your intruder may die as a result of the fight, but that isn't your immediate concern. Your focus needs to be on stopping his attack. If at the first sight of determined resistance he decides to break off his attack and run away, you've won! Do not pursue him in a misguided attempt to capture him or extract some sort of payback. Let him go. By pursuing, you expose yourself to greater danger and substantially increase the risk of turning a straightforward self-defense case into a legal mess. If he stops, you stop.

Giving yourself and your family permission to fight is an important step. Our society operates because we (by and large) treat each other with respect. It can be a difficult transition for some people, particularly children, to engage in violence against another human being. In the Adaptive Personal Security model, we work to avoid confrontation through Deterrence and Detection. But sometimes that's not enough. Righteous violence needs to be a consideration in your planning.

If you have dedicated weapons staged, such as defensive firearms, those are your most efficient choices against a lethal threat. If you've chosen to have a home-defense firearm, it's important to understand when you can and cannot use it against an intruder. The books ***Deadly Force by Massad Ayoob*** and the aforementioned ***The Law of Self Defense by Andrew Branca*** are highly recommended.

Back to Anticipation

Make sure you have plans to regularly rehearse your Response, just as you might plan fire drills. Put them into your matrix as Maintenance items, and make sure you update the matrix with the date of the next planned rehearsal.

THE SEVERE TRAUMA EMERGENCY

Those of us who study and teach self-defense (in my case, defensive shooting) often suffer from a form of myopia. As a group, we seem unable (or possibly unwilling) to see past our own biases and preconceptions and look at the "big picture."

One of those blind spots has to do with severe trauma — particularly life-threatening blood loss. This kind of injury is far more common than the need to use lethal force, and until just a few years ago, nearly everyone ignored the reality. But today, trauma kits and the training to use them are part of most instructors' teaching gear.

This hasn't yet filtered down to the general public, and it's a shame. Severe, life-threatening blood loss is a common result of many kinds of accidents every day in this country. As one prepared individual once told me, "I've never needed to use my gun to defend my life, but I've used my trauma kit three times to save lives."

Severe blood loss can occur in many kinds of accidents, some of them almost trivially common. Car accidents often result in life-threatening hemorrhaging, and more than one victim has "bled out" before paramedics could arrive on scene. Industrial accidents, especially with saws, are another risk. Children falling through windows and drunks putting their fists through windows often result in severe bleeding, and bow hunters are a slipped step away from a deadly broadhead wound.

If you're still more concerned about a criminal attack, think about this: Knife and bullet wounds often result in life-threatening bleeding. You might drop the bad guy in his tracks with your gun, but the wounds you sustained can make that a short-lived victory if not attended to immediately. Knowing how to stop your own hemorrhaging may be what saves your life.

Worried about terrorist attacks? Again, bullet wounds are dangerous — but so are severed limbs from bombs. The current favorite terrorist tactic, using a vehicle to run people down, results in multiple victims whose wound profiles are much like those of auto accident victims.

No matter what threats you're worried about, they almost all carry the risk of death from severe trauma. Knowing how to handle it is really the universal survival preparation!

Getting trauma training

I don't teach trauma response, but I recommend everyone take a trauma course before taking a defensive shooting course. (That's probably why I'm not yet rich from my defensive shooting teaching — I'm undercutting my own market!) Since severe trauma is so deadly yet so common, it ranks higher by my own measure (incidence versus consequence) than self-defense with a firearm. It's something everyone should prepare for.

Where do you find this kind of training? Well, your local Red Cross is most assuredly NOT the place to start! The Red Cross is great for teaching the Heimlich Maneuver and CPR, but when it comes to trauma response, their approach is to throw up their hands and tell you to call 9-1-1.

Instead, look for a class near you offered by someone with trauma response experience. Most of these instructors are ex-military medics, where the doctrine of handling trauma is currently state-of-the-art.*

You'll also find some EMTs and Paramedics who work for progressive agencies using modern methods, and they teach courses on the side.

Most of these courses have names like Tactical Combat Casualty Care (TCCC) and Tactical Emergency Casualty Care (TECC), the latter being the civilian version of the former. They all fall under the umbrella term "tactical medicine."

These courses revolve around teaching you how to stabilize a patient and get him/her ready for transport to an emergency department. They usually teach how to apply tourniquets, use hemostatic (blood clotting) materials, and how to handle perforating chest wounds. Frequently included is information on how to handle airway obstructions and prevent shock. If the instructor is properly prepared, there will be plenty of hands-on practice of each of these techniques throughout the course.

What to look for

Most of the courses I've seen and attended have been one-day affairs, though two-day courses are becoming more common. I found one day was more than sufficient to learn the basic concepts and participate in sufficient skill-building exercises. Some of the courses are very militaristic and have a distinctly masculine approach, while others are more suitable for family learning.

Shop carefully. I've found ex-military medics to lean toward the masculine end, while civilian EMTs and Paramedics tend to be less so. This is not always true, of course, and there is no substitute for talking with your teacher beforehand.

If your prospective instructor is ex-military, you want to see recent, verifiable credentials as an active-duty medic (or higher). If he or she is a civilian, you want them to have graduated from the Tactical Emergency Casualty Care (TECC) program offered through the National Association of Emergency Medical Technicians (NAEMT).

The trauma kit

In addition to learning how to treat severe trauma, you should also put together (or buy) a trauma kit to carry with you. While I'm not dogmatic about many things, in this case I am: You should always carry a trauma kit with you. Severe trauma is so common, so ubiquitous, and so dangerous that I believe everyone should be equipped with both the skills and tools to deal with it.

A trauma response kit isn't a suitcase-sized bag full of EMT gear. A functional minimalist kit consists of a tourniquet, hemostatic gauze or sponge, pressure bandage, and perhaps a chest seal. This kit takes up little room but has the capability of saving someone's life — perhaps even your own!

How do you carry it? I carry mine in my ever-present messenger bag (along with various other things I consider important to my multi-threat Response plans). If you carry a purse, you can probably find room for these items. A briefcase is also a natural way to carry your kit.

Kits are available that have been vacuum-packed to take up little space, and easily fit in a coat or cargo pocket. If your wardrobe allows it, an ankle band — such as this one from Safer Faster Defense — designed specifically to carry medical equipment may be your solution.

Yes, I feel strongly about this! If you look at the threats you've identified in your life, you'll probably see a lot of them have the potential for severe life-threatening trauma. Learning and equipping yourself to deal with it is perhaps the most universal preparation you can make.

Be sure to inspect your trauma kit regularly. Use the Maintain space in your matrix to schedule the necessary inspections.

---

* — *This is one area where the military is well beyond most EMT and Paramedic courses. It's a matter of historical record that war always results in medical advancements, and our decades-long involvement in the various Middle East conflicts has greatly increased our knowledge of emergency medicine.*

FIRES: HOME AND WILD

Amazingly, when I talk to people about either preparedness or self-defense, the subject of fire survival rarely comes up. Fires, whether they're in your home or in the forest next to your house, are certainly life-altering events. They can destroy everything you've worked for, and they kill people. Every year in this country, fires kill over 3,000 people and result in over $13 billion in losses.

That's something you might want to prepare for. Of course fire prevention falls easily into your Deter planning, and fire alarms into Detect. What about Respond — have you thought about what to do if a fire breaks out?

The fire drill

I'm sure you participated in fire drills at school. Have you done them at home? If not, remedy that immediately! The fire drill ingrains proper Response. When your smoke detectors wake you in the middle of the night, as they often do, your rehearsed Response is what is likely to save you.

Of course you need to think through all the various ways and places fires can start in order to plan your best escape routes. Make sure you do, and that you've practiced them before you need them. Make those practice or drill sessions part of the Maintenance entry in your matrixes.

Have a bailout kit packed and ready to go

We'll discuss pre-staging survival kits in a later chapter, but think for a minute what you'd do if you had to get out of your house during a fire. Your kids might be wearing only pajamas. Most adults are likely to be wearing considerably less. Perhaps you grab a bathrobe on the way out. If the fire is in the middle of winter, you'll be stuck without clothing suitable for the weather. You might also be without clothing for the next day or so. What about your medications?

Bailout kits aren't just for big natural disasters. They're useful, and perhaps more plausibly useful, for mundane emergencies like this. On your way out, grab your emergency bag. At least you'll be prepared for short-term survival while you arrange to put your life back together.

Wildfires

Those who live in areas where wildfires are a threat should always be prepared for an evacuation. Whether in the forest or the desert grasslands, wildfires destroy homes and businesses and kill people on a regular basis. Fire officials monitor the speed and direction of the flame front and evacuate homes in the fire's path. These pre-emptive evacuations save lives.

However, you need to give some thought to just how you'd evacuate if given the order. Being orderly and efficient minimizes not only your losses, but also the impact on your life. It may even mean the difference between escaping unharmed and suffering serious injury while fleeing.

(Mandatory evacuations carry the force of law in most jurisdictions, though penalties are rarely enforced.* If you refuse to leave, there's little the authorities are likely to do, but it may come down to exercising your right to be stupid. If the situation is so dire that people are being asked to vacate the area, your own internal goal to protect your life should compel you to leave without being forced!)

Of course you should take with you those things you need to maintain a reasonably comfortable life. Because evacuations generally give you some time — though it may be as short as an hour — you'll be able to do more than just grab a bag and run.

Plan ahead for how and what you'd do in an evacuation. It's helpful to have an evacuation checklist prepared and ordered in terms of priority. The more time you have, the farther down the list you'll be able to proceed. Making sure the high-priority items are at the top ensures they'll get done no matter how little time you have.

Involve as many family members in the evacuation procedure as possible. If you have small children who can't help, make sure they're secured in your evacuation vehicle before you do anything else, and check on them frequently.

This type of evacuation planning is valuable for other types of disasters as well.

*www.americanbar.org/publications/law_practice_today_home/law_practice_t oday_archive/april11/fight_or_flight_on_enforcing_mandatory_evacuations.ht ml

NATURAL AND MAN-MADE DISASTERS

This is something of a "catch-all" chapter, because a wide range of life-altering events may share some of the same Response planning.

Your own personal disaster

A lot of events can impact your life but won't make the evening news. I call these "private disasters," because they threaten you and you alone. You need to prepare to Respond to those just as much as you prepare to Respond to events that affect your whole town or state.

What constitutes a private disaster? Let's say your car breaks down on a rural road 10 miles from home and your cell phone battery is dead. What might your Response be? If you're like most people, you'll start hiking. To do so, you need water and good shoes. Are you ready?

What if it's cold and wet? Add in rain gear and a warm coat. What if it's very hot? How are you going to prevent heat exhaustion? How about at night?

What if it's not a car breakdown, but instead you've slid off the road in the snow and your car isn't visible?

You can see how even a small event, one that very few people would ever think twice about, can turn serious. A few years ago, not far from where I live, a couple and their two children mistakenly followed their GPS "shortcut" onto a little-used Forest Service road. They got stuck in the snow miles from the nearest house. The father decided to hike out and get help, leaving his wife and children in the car.

Their next reunion was at his funeral. He died of exposure because he wasn't equipped to make such a hike in those conditions. Tragic, but it shows how quickly a minor annoyance can turn into a life-threatening event. I can hear your protestations now: "I'm much smarter than that! It could never happen to me!" This fellow was very smart too; an accomplished engineer, in fact. Belief in their own invincibility leads people to do dangerous things, not lack of intelligence. It also causes people not to prepare in the first place.

This is why I call these private disasters: They may indeed threaten your life or the lives of your immediate loved ones, and they're something for which you should prepare.

Widespread events

When we think of the word "disaster," we usually think of widespread events, the kind that do make the news: hurricanes, tornadoes, multi-state winter storms, earthquakes, and the like. "Disaster" brings to mind Mother Nature and "acts of God." As I write this, thousands of citizens downstream of a dam in California are being evacuated because record rainfall has resulted in damage that threatens the dam's failure. They're being forced to flee their homes, and I'm willing to bet almost none of them have ever planned for this kind of event.

Disasters aren't just about the weather. They can be manmade events as well, the result of failure, accident, or even sabotage. A train derailment with overturned chemical tank cars can cause the evacuation of an entire town. If the tanks catch fire, the threat can spread to wherever the prevailing winds blow. Manmade systems that aren't resilient to natural events combined with normal human mistakes can turn horrific in mere minutes, as the Fukushima nuclear disaster in 2011 showed us.

There are several differences between the personal and the public disaster. The first is you won't be alone. A lot of people will be sharing in your hardships and facing the same potential for personal loss. The problem is all of those co-victims are a huge drain on available Response resources. Resource depletion can happen even before the event begins, as news reports of bare store shelves in advance of major storms clearly illustrate.

Ironically, you may be more on your own in a public disaster than a private one, because there may be no preparation, rescue, or recovery resources left. This underscores the fallacy of relying on other people for your security or waiting until the last moment to prepare. (I would hope, if you've read this far, you're not such a person!)

The sheer number of people affected by a widespread disaster is likely to impede your ability to get away from the threat. It's not uncommon, particularly in evacuation situations, for roads to become helplessly clogged. If your plans include "bugging out" (more on that later), you may not be able to go anywhere. You may not be able to make it home to your family, or they may not be able to make it home to be with you. How resilient is your planning for those scenarios?

Finally, it's possible the people suffering with you might become secondary threats themselves. It's easy to find cases where people have come together and unselfishly helped each other to survive their shared crisis. Sadly, it's also fairly easy to find cases where people turned on each other to fight over scarce resources like food and shelter. Sometimes you can find both happening in the same event, depending on how much neighborhood cohesion existed prior to the event.

I understand the reticence most people have to think ill of those suffering with them. I too find it hard to think the worst of my fellow man, and I don't want you to automatically assume the worst of everyone. But the reality is, your neighbors may not prove to be allies unless you do some preparatory work now to make sure they are. Get to know your neighbors and involve them in cooperative events. Even something as simple as a neighborhood yard sale each spring may be enough to bring people out of their shells and see their neighbors as friends and allies.

If you don't know your neighbors and if your community doesn't seem to have the kind of cohesion that would help them survive a severe emergency, this kind of relationship building needs to be a part of your Adaptive Personal Security planning. Never underestimate the power of people allied for a common cause.

Hope for the best, but prepare for the worst.

DEALING WITH A PUBLIC ATTACK

Public attacks, whether due to terrorism or your garden-variety malcontent, grab headlines all over the world. While these events are quite rare, our modern 24-hour news cycle makes it seem like they happen constantly. You should be concerned about them, but not to the point of paranoia. As with any other frightening event, having a Response plan ahead of time helps reduce your anxiety and markedly increases your chances of escaping unharmed.

The active shooter

Foremost in people's minds is probably the active shooter: the person or small group who attacks a larger group in public using firearms. Their aim is usually to inflict a maximum number of casualties in a short span of time before being caught or killed by law enforcement.

Active shooters come in all varieties. Some are religiously motivated, others politically. In our country, many active shooters are disaffected teenagers with a history of emotional or psychological issues. Still others are fired employees out to extract revenge on their boss and former co-workers. Why they do it isn't really important, because the Response is about the act, not the reason.

Without a Response plan, you'll see people either freeze, not knowing what to do, or react unpredictably — perhaps placing themselves in even greater danger. In the past, the recommendation was basically to "hide and hope": to cower in a corner and hope the bad guy doesn't find you. This approach has a history of poor outcomes, and as we've learned, there are better things victims of an active shooter can do to raise their survival odds.

Today, we teach a process that is similar to the home and family defense Response:

- Evade
- Barricade
- Arm yourself
- Communicate
- Fight (if necessary)

In public, as opposed to in your home, these components take on a slightly different meaning, but the principles are the same. Keep in mind these are not intended to be orders of operation, but rather functions that you bring into use as necessary or appropriate.

Evade

If you can do so safely, immediately exit the area. Don't wait around to find out what the threat is or to rubberneck. If you hear gunshots, find a safe direction to leave.

Many times people run for the exits in a building only to find the attacker is between them and the exit. This brings them closer to the threat and can result in casualties. If you're going to leave, in general you want to leave by going in the opposite direction from the attacker(s).

In a mall, there will be exits beside the doors through which you entered. Virtually all merchants in a mall have a back door that accesses a freight/service corridor. The hallway usually leads to a loading dock or freight area. When a shooter opens fire, if you can't see an exit, it's best to head into the closest store and straight for the back door.

(Sometimes those corridors have a secondary outlet into the mall area itself. Don't burst through a door without first checking to see what's on the other side — it could open directly in front of the shooter!)

If you're with your family, gather and herd them in the safest direction. You may need to pick up your kids and carry them. Don't be shy about doing so, even if they're of an age where you don't normally pick them up. If they show any hesitation, grab them and go.

Again, the purpose of evasion is to make yourself safer by getting away from the threat. Anytime you enter a building, take note of where the exits are. Are they locked? Are they in an "employees only" area?

I read recently about a school evacuation drill where students were going through a double door in single file because a sign on one of the doors said "Use other door"! In an emergency, ignore "authorized personnel only" signs.

Locating those areas and deciding ahead of time that you'll violate the restrictive signs prime your mind for action in the event of an attack. Without that, you might be caught reflexively obeying the signs like the kids in the school evacuation!

Get into the habit of looking for exits wherever you go. This habit is useful for a wide variety of threats, including fire. (While you're at it, look where the fire extinguishers are located — not only are they useful for putting out fires, they make dandy improvised weapons as well!)

Always think about how you'd get out safely if a situation required you to leave in a hurry. If you can't find a safe way out, you may need to go to "Plan B": barricade.

Barricade

In a home invasion Response, barricading should be fairly easy: You go to your pre-arranged safe space that you've set up to be defensible. In a public space, you don't have the luxury of a preplanned area, so you need to look for a suitable place.

By barricade, I don't mean just hiding under a table or behind a trash can. A barricaded position is one that is both securable and defensible. "Securable" means it can be locked or otherwise structured to make it difficult for the attacker to gain access. A storage closet with a steel door and deadbolt is an ideal barricaded position: The attacker doesn't know you're there and can't easily get to you.

"Defensible" means it's arranged (or you've arranged it yourself) in such a way that if the attacker did make entry, you could mount an effective counter-attack. If you're in the storage closet and there's a place to hide at a right angle to the doorway, if your attacker manages to get the door open, he won't see you immediately — giving you the opportunity to surprise him with a defensive attack.

Look for a place where you can deny an attacker entry and be able to defend yourself effectively. A useful exercise whenever you're in a public space is to pay attention to possible barricade areas. Which doors have locks on them? What would be hard to break into? What would shield you from bullets? Make it part of your routine to look for exits. It only takes seconds and can be done without calling attention to yourself. All you have to do is pay attention.

Arm yourself

If you're not already armed when an attack happens, and you can't get away safely, you should look around for weapons in your environment. As mentioned in the section on home defense, look around for things that stab, slice, bludgeon, or distract. I mentioned fire extinguishers, and thanks to fire laws and building codes, they are ubiquitous in public areas. So much so that people routinely ignore them! You shouldn't. Not only might you need one in case of fire, but you might also press one into service during an attack.

You may find lots of other potential weapons if you just look for them and think not in terms of what they're normally used for, but how much damage they might do if intentionally misused. Your job is, in fact, to misuse them to your greatest advantage!

Communicate

In the context of a public attack, communication means two things. First, you need to communicate to the authorities an attack is happening. The better witness you are, the more information responding officers have to effectively deal with the attacker(s).

Tell the dispatch operator where the attack is occurring, where you are barricaded, how many attackers you know of, how they're armed, and so on. Give good descriptions whenever possible, and indicate how many casualties you are aware of.

Just as for a home invasion drill, it's useful to practice how you'd talk to 9-1-1 in an emergency. Most people don't give the operators good information, often spending time on irrelevancies or speculations. Practicing ahead of time, even pretending to speak to an operator, will help you keep your mind on the task in a real incident. Practice giving the dispatcher the essential information, starting with the address, and do so in a logical manner. It speeds up response!

It's also important to communicate with those around you. If you're in a room with several people, you need to coordinate your actions should the attacker make it into your barricaded space. Talk with them and indicate what you'll do and what you think they should do — someone with a head on their shoulders needs to be in the leadership position, and that person may be you.

Again, this is worth practicing ahead of time with your family playing the other victims.

Fight (if necessary)

Your decision to fight might occur because you can't evade safely and an attacker confronts you before you can barricade, it might happen because you've decided to fight instead of trying to get away, or it might occur because the attacker made it through your barricade and now you have no choice. Whatever the case, if it's necessary to fight, it's necessary to do everything you can to prevail! Use the weapons you have with you and use things in your environment to distract, delay, or disable your attacker. If you're in a group and someone has given you an opening to counter-attack, taking the opening may be preferable to cowering in the corner and waiting for the bad guy to kill you.

Decide now that you'll do whatever is necessary to prevail against your attacker. With that decision pre-made, all you have to do is choose your weapons and mount your defense.

Should you engage an active shooter?

This is a topic of great debate among concealed-carry teachers and advocates: Should you use your concealed handgun to engage an active shooter? There is no hard and fast answer to the question. It's going to depend on the circumstances of the attack, but also your belief in your own skills and the amount of risk you're willing to assume. There have been incidents where an active shooter has been successfully engaged by someone with a concealed weapon, and other cases where the person was injured or killed for his trouble.

If you're single, you might answer this differently than if you're married with children. I would argue your first obligation is always to your family, and you should do whatever is necessary to make sure they're safe and that you return home to them. If it means leaving the attacker to someone else while you evade safely, I suggest that be your decision.

If you decide to engage the attacker, do not tell him to drop his gun or surrender. That's Hollywood nonsense. If he's shooting and killing people, you have no legal or moral obligation to put yourself at risk by identifying yourself to the killer. Do what's necessary to incapacitate him. Be aware he may not be the only shooter, and you may get shot by his accomplice for your trouble. Active shooters are a complex situation to handle, which is why they're so dangerous to begin with.

Think about this ahead of time, preferably in your Anticipation planning. Visualize the scenarios where you would and would not intervene, but only after considering your family.

Bomb attacks

The public bombing is a very different kind of attack. Unless you're well trained to spot the cues, or the attackers are particularly inept, your first indication of a bomb attack is likely to be the explosion itself.

What if, by sheer chance, you happen to spot someone you think is wearing a bomb or placing one? Your first reaction must be to get as far away as possible, as quickly as possible. Despite what you see on television, bombs kill at surprisingly long distances. The flying shrapnel from the bomb itself, combined with the debris it creates from its immediate surroundings, can injure or kill at long distances. The shockwave from the bomb can also cause severe injuries at surprising range.

If you suspect a bomb, get out of its path and as far away as possible. If you can put solid barriers between you and the device, do so — but don't stop to hide behind a barrier. Put something between you and the bomb and keep moving directly away.

As I said, your first indication of a bomb is most likely going to be its explosion. If you're lucky enough to remain ambulatory, you need to get to safety. Buildings collapse after bomb blasts, and while that is certainly a hazard, a more urgent concern is the possibility of a secondary device. Bombers have learned to plant their devices in such a way as to cause a great number of casualties, then they set off a second device to kill the first responders, survivors, onlookers, and Good Samaritans. If one bomb goes off, assume a second will detonate within a few minutes.

Savvy bombers place the secondary devices where people are likely to congregate after the first blast. This is a time when going with the flow of traffic is a very bad idea. If you see the crowd moving in one direction, it's a safe bet they're heading toward the secondary device without realizing it. Go in the opposite direction, toward an area with few people. It's unlikely the attacker will waste another device on an empty loading dock, for example.

These decisions you make in advance prime your mind, leaving you to simply execute the action when the time comes. Understanding how attacks in public happen is the first step in deciding what you'll do if you need to.

BUGGING OUT AND BUGGING IN

The preparedness community sometimes seems fixated on the concept of "bugging out": leaving your home with survival supplies on your back and heading for an often vague retreat location. Even a quick web search will net you many articles on bugging out, bugout bags and kits, and how to prepare a bugout retreat.

Sometimes it's necessary to leave your home due to a disaster, but not always. I think hardcore survivalists sometimes romanticize the notion of rugged individualism to the point they lose sight of reality. Let's have a look at what bugging out entails.

Why would you bug out?

To start with a basic question: Why would you ever want to bug out? The usual scenario offered by proponents of the idea is an apocalyptic one. Your home has been rendered uninhabitable by some means, and the danger is so great that you must vacate the entire area (neighborhood or even city).

What events could cause such a catastrophe? A devastating flood is one, or perhaps a tremendous release of chemical or nuclear materials.

All have happened and required the large-scale relocation of the affected populations.

A favorite of the survivalist crowd is the rather ill-defined "civil unrest": gangs of roving brigands who drive out the legitimate population, or organized military units bent on enslaving the citizens against their will. It's possible to find cases of this happening in third-world countries and banana republics, but it's a pretty far-fetched notion for most of us.

Whatever the reason, the disaster supposedly causes you to evacuate quickly, with only what you can carry on your back. In this scenario, proponents of the bugout believe, you'd retreat to a defensible area and live off the land until society stabilizes and it becomes safe to go back to civilization. More pragmatic survivalists recognize that living off the land is impractical in the extreme, and instead propose a pre-stocked survival retreat to which you go to weather the fall of society.

What do you need to bug out?

What you need depends on how pragmatic you are. If you're the idealistic type, you need enough food and water so you can hike to a wilderness area where you can hide out and harvest game. If you're a bit more realistic, you need to reach your pre-staged retreat where you can hide out and wait for the end of the world.

I think both are incredibly naive.

The wilderness option

Let's start with the notion that you'll be able to retreat to the woods and live off what you can hunt and trap. First, of course, you need to get there. You either need to drive a long distance to the wilderness or hike there. If the scenario is so dire you need to leave your home and escape, no doubt others will have the same idea to flee as well. Roads are likely to be hopelessly clogged. Look what happens during the mildest of winter storms all over this country.

You've got a four-wheel-drive vehicle and plan to just go across country? Even a 4WD won't take you across deep rivers or significant obstacles (either natural or manmade). At some point, you'll need to cross over private property. How happy do you think the locals will be at some out-of-towner tearing down their fences and putting ruts in their fields? Your 4x4 will, at best, let you get out of the traffic on the interstate and onto a backroad — where you're likely to find the same problem.

Of course you need enough fuel for your thirsty vehicle to reach your destination. If the incident is so widespread you need to bug out, you're unlikely to get fuel resupply along the way. That means you need to carry it with you, which means starting with a full tank and full auxiliary containers. Right now, at this moment, how full is the tank in your vehicle? Where are your auxiliary fuel containers?

If you're planning to hike, how experienced a hiker are you? How far can you carry a 50-pound load under realistic (i.e., cross-country with no trails) conditions? It's not easy to do even for someone in good shape. If you're only in average condition, you won't make it very far each day. If, like me, you're well past fifty years of age, you might be surprised how quickly you tire even with a light load.

Hiking means carrying everything you need to start a new (if only temporary) life. You need to carry food and water to get to your destination, and when you get there, you need to immediately start hunting and foraging for food. An expert woodsperson might be able to do it, but just how experienced are you? Hunting and foraging are great for a snack after a refreshing hike. They're something else entirely when you need to be successful to survive.

A big influx of like-minded people into your area will quickly deplete the local game population. Depending on the environment, even a few families could rapidly reduce the living protein populations to almost nothing. You're probably thinking that if the deer are gone, you can still live off squirrels and other small animals. I can tell you a single squirrel doesn't go very far, especially when one is hungry. You're unlikely to find enough of them to fill your protein needs over a long period of time, especially in the winter.

Do I need to ask how experienced a hunter you are?

You also need to build a long-term shelter. You can't live in a tent forever, because they quickly wear out — especially in severe weather. How easy is it to build a log cabin? I've done it, and I can tell you "not very darned easy," even with power tools. How will you heat it — did you bring a woodstove with you? Masonry tools?

This is just scratching the surface of the issues you'll face trying to bug out to a wilderness area. There's something else to remember — no matter where you go in this country, you'll likely need to deal with the locals who already live there. In a widespread disaster, they're not going to be terribly keen on new people moving in and taking "their" game from the woods. Unless you're camped out in a state or federal forest, someone owns that land. How welcoming will the landowners be when they find squatters on their property?

As a rural resident and owner of a woodland, I wouldn't be terribly happy about the prospect. My neighbors would likely encourage interlopers to move on to somewhere else, and they wouldn't be nearly as nice about it as I would!

Pre-planning your retreat

One way around some of these issues is to establish a retreat before you need to bug out. This is a popular notion with a wide range of survivalists, and is often the central feature of much of the "prepper fiction" that's written about the end of the world. The idea is to buy or build a rural retreat and keep it stocked with everything you'll need to ride out the collapse of society.

This option is, naturally, quite expensive. You'll have two mortgages, plus the cost of building and stocking what amounts to a second household. The very wealthy do it (more often than you might believe), but for most people it's financially impossible.

A big problem with the prepared retreat plan is security — keeping everything from being stolen before you get there. A few prepper retreats are in my neck of the woods, and most (if not all) have been burglarized. Many have been hit more than once and have had squatters living in them. Some have been turned into drug labs, and the resulting hazmat cleanup caused their owners no end of expense.

Let's say you have the money and have arranged for continuous security on your rural retreat. You still have the problem of getting there, and it's the same problem as the person who plans to bug out to the wilderness. The locals won't be all that fond of you, either. Unlike squatters, you'll be tolerated, but that's about the extent of what you can expect.

Unless you've consciously worked to make friends beforehand, don't expect help from your neighbors. Folks in the country tend to be quite cliquish and resent "rich out-of-towners."

(I personally know of a retreat owned by a famous and somewhat arrogant actor whose neighbors greatly resented his presence in their sparsely populated area. He finally sold the property after realizing he needed their help if his family were ever to survive there, but they were never going to accept him. It doesn't take a famous name to receive the same treatment. Out-of-towners of all kinds often face similar issues.)

Outside of the security issues, a retreat needs to be maintained. As any vacation homeowner can attest, a building that's not being lived in quickly deteriorates. Moisture rots wood and causes mold and mildew, water pipes freeze and crack (or corrode), and heating systems fail. Some people pay to continuously heat their vacation homes, which only adds to the financial burden. Others rent out their vacation homes to keep a steady flow of people in and out, but it's a serious risk for a bugout retreat. What do you do with renters who won't leave because they just discovered they have nothing to go back to?

The bugout retreat is more pipe dream than practicality for most of us.

The lessons of refugees

One thing to keep in mind is that, if you don't have a specific place to go, bugging out essentially turns you into a refugee. Even if you're headed for a pre-planned retreat, the trip there (particularly if it involves a long hike) turns you into a temporary refugee.

I've met many people who have been refugees from war, political turmoil, and natural and manmade disasters. All of them say being a refugee is the most dangerous and dehumanizing experience of their lives. Refugees are at the mercy of either the relief agencies tasked with helping them or the criminals who prey on them — sometimes both. Anything you can do to avoid exposing yourself to the stream of people trying to get to safety greatly aids your personal security.

There are some alternatives to consider.

Alternative One: bugging in

Look back to your threat list and think about the kinds of things that would cause you to abandon your home. I'll bet you find, in most cases, you'd be better served by staying right where you are rather than trying to get away. The concept is known as "bugging in."

Very few events would necessitate you leaving your home because of a proximate danger. If your home were destroyed — by fire, earthquake, flood, tornado, etc. — you'd probably need to abandon it. But what about all the other kinds of incidents? For many of them, staying put may be your best option. It's also the first one you should probably prepare for.

Your home is your greatest source of sustenance. It has all your food, tools, and defensive arrangements, not to mention it keeps you dry and warm. Why not plan to take advantage of that by staying there if at all possible?

Even if your home proper is destroyed, bugging in on your own property may still be a more viable option that hightailing it for the hills. Once it passes, an earthquake poses little further threat. You can camp out in your backyard as repairs are made to your home or as you arrange for other shelter. Running with your neighbors to a community shelter that may be overcrowded and dangerous is, in my mind, less preferable than sleeping in a tent.

Think through all the disaster scenarios that fit the threat profile you've made. How many of them really require you to leave your neighborhood? How many of them could be easily addressed by bugging in?

Alternative Two: doubling up

An alternative not often discussed is to pre-arrange to stay with friends or relatives who live out of your immediate area. In case your home is destroyed or made truly uninhabitable, you have a pre-arranged, pre-stocked, and already secured place to go. It might involve living in a guest room, sleeping on a couch, or temporarily sheltering in a garage, but it's a significant upgrade to trying to live in the woods!

This alternative gives you everything the fully stocked retreat gives the rich: prearranged food, shelter, and infrastructure that's been maintained and is fully operational. It also gives you an advantage the rural retreat doesn't have, which is a pre-existing relationship with the locals. Staying with friends or family allows you to take advantage of their local relationships. You're not as much of an interloper when you're staying with someone they already know!

You'll also have built-in support, and your friends/relatives will gain support from you. Having an extra set of hands to help out with the increased chores is always appreciated, and having an emotional support system at hand is a big aid in maintaining your sanity during a long-term crisis.

Of course you need to discuss this with your friends or family ahead of time — don't just show up expecting to be let in! Prearranging to double up means that you contribute to an emergency food stock everyone will use during the event. It means pre-placing some of your own possessions in their attic or basement, ready for use when you arrive.

It also means helping them with their personal security and preparedness planning. Now that you've adopted a rational and systematic plan for yourself, you can "pay it forward" and use your knowledge to help them become safer and more resilient. It can even become a mutual hobby, with each helping the other and sharing what they've learned and done.

It should go without saying this arrangement is two-way. While you're planning to visit them if you can't live in your house any longer, they'll be planning to do the same thing at your house. This gives each of you a welcoming and prepared place to bug out if you really need to. It's a little like getting two for the price of one!

Alternative Three: the mobile bugout

As already mentioned, bugging in is probably a more realistic option for a wide range of disasters. If your home is damaged to the point that it's unlivable, from events such as a fire or earthquake, you'll need shelter — but you may not need to leave the area.

If you have the space for it, a small travel trailer may be a good solution. It can be parked next to or behind your garage and it carries in it all the creature comforts of home (albeit on a much smaller scale). If your home is rendered uninhabitable, you move into your travel trailer while you make repairs or more permanent arrangements for a place to live.

The travel trailer should be fully stocked with food, clothing, and sundries. A good tactic is to use the travel trailer as your pantry to store additional food and supplies. This makes it both storage and retreat and keeps things properly rotated.

A travel trailer is in some ways much like a house, in that it can deteriorate if it's not kept heated during the cold or damp months. Luckily their small space doesn't require much to heat to a maintenance level. My parents, who owned such a trailer for many years, kept a small ceramic heater running during those months. As a result, their trailer was never musty nor developed any mold or mildew. It was a very small monthly expense that kept their trailer in like-new condition long after it was manufactured.

The mobile retreat may also be taken to another location if it's necessary to leave. Of course you're still at the mercy of jammed traffic, but the trailer gives you the ability to "time shift" your departure. This means you can leave after the worst of the traffic jams have been cleared. If you find yourself on the highway and traffic becomes impassable, you can just pull off the road and camp while you wait for things to clear out.

A travel trailer is likely to be more expensive than doubling up, but is considerably cheaper and more flexible than maintaining a fixed retreat somewhere. It also gives you travel options that neither of the other alternatives does, as you can easily go in the opposite direction of your plans if needed.

Of course there is always Alternative Four: All of the above!

EMERGENCY KITS FOR EVERY NEED

Survival kits are a big topic in both the self-defense and preparedness worlds. Kits are collections of essential items contained in something that makes the whole thing easy to transport. You'll hear and see references to 72-hour kits, bug-out bags, get-home bags, along with numerous permutations and variations.

These kits all have one thing in common: They allow you to make it through a short, fixed period of time when outside aid or supply is inconvenient, unlikely, or impossible. A kit may be as simple as a regular selection of things you carry in your pockets or purse, or as complex as multiple waterproof stacking containers.

An internet search turns up all kinds of "survival porn": detailed pictures of kits, their contents, and what they're carried in. For some people, those pictures (often accompanied by breathless descriptions) of what others have in their kits initiates a kind of "keeping up with the Joneses" race. It's common to see people adding things to their kits because someone else has that item — with little or no thought to the utility and logistical issues that come with an ever-growing bag of "stuff."

I encourage you to make kits appropriate to your life and the dangers you face. But make sure those kits make sense for you and not someone else.

Some kit considerations

The whole idea of a kit is to have a portable selection of items to help you survive, in the best possible condition, some sort of emergency. Any survival kit is really a subset of the preparedness items you have at home. The kit suffices to keep you healthy (and possibly happy) when you aren't able to access your home-based resources. Whether it's because the event has prevented you from getting home or has forced you to leave your home, your kits should have sufficient items to enable you to reach a safer space.

Don't overload

The key to any kit, and the first consideration you need to make, is its portability. Think about how you'll transport your kit. Whether it's to get you home or to a safe space other than home, you'll need to take the kit with you. This is something a lot of people seem to overlook!

When designing a portable kit, be honest about your own physical limitations. I've seen many bug-out bags that weighed 40 pounds or more. As I mentioned earlier, are you really in shape to carry a 40-pound backpack for any distance — particularly if the terrain is rough or there is an uphill slope?

How you transport your kit has a huge bearing on what you put in it. If you live in a wildfire area, you likely need to be prepared for an evacuation with some prior notice. In such a case, you'll probably be using a vehicle and your evacuation kit can simply be in plastic totes that slide into your minivan. On the other hand, if your main fire concern is getting out of the house with some clothes to wear while you find a motel, your evac kits need to be small, easily carried out a window, and quickly grabbed.

A wildfire evacuation kit will more than likely be transported by car. It would seem weight wouldn't be much of an issue, but it is. What if those plastic totes are loaded to a weight the husky husband can easily lift, but the evacuation order comes while he's at work — and his petite wife is left with the task of lifting those into the trunk of her car? Think about how you'll be moving it, but just as importantly who will be moving it.

Consider every family member

If you're going to make any sort of emergency kit, remember it's not just about you. Each family member's needs must be met by your kit(s), but the kits need to stay with them. Teenagers can probably carry their own, but your toddlers can't. You'll need to carry your stuff and theirs, which means you'll need to pay very close attention to what goes into the kit. You can't carry everything and you may need to make some painful choices.

You'll also need to revisit the kits over time as your children grow. Not only will they be able to shoulder more of the burden as they age, but the things they need will change as well. After a while you don't need to worry about diapers, but may need to worry about feminine hygiene products.

While you're at it, consider what your kids will need to have with them as they go off to college or spend long periods of the summer at camp. They need an emergency kit then, too, and if you've raised them with a self-reliant attitude, they'll find it normal to take one with them. Sit down with them and talk about the environment they'll be in, what kinds of emergencies might happen, and how their kit needs to change from the one they have at home. Make those changes, always with an eye toward portability. Ensure your kids always have on hand the things (and associated skills) they'll need to keep safe no matter where they are.

Keep in mind that with kids, packaging might be everything. A child who doesn't want to carry one of "Dad's stupid Army bags" may be amenable to toting something more fashionable among his/her peer group. This has the additional benefit of helping the child maintain a low profile while out and about, reducing his/her chances of being noticed and targeted.

If you're of the age where multiple medications are the order of the day, or someone in your family is, you'll need to add those to your kit contents. (Be sure to regularly check the expiration dates.)

(This should be a lesson for you, too. Looking like Rambo but working in a stylish uptown office is a great way to get noticed, perhaps by the wrong people. Your emergency kit needs to fit in with your lifestyle as well!)

There's a certain amount of overlap in the kits recommended by various preparedness "experts." Read through them and decide what's right for you.

Kits for every situation

You'll likely end up with several kits to address various needs. You might need one kit to deal with a house fire, another kit to deal with your car being stranded, and perhaps another if the family is forced to abandon your home.

But not everyone needs many different kits, and the kind of kit(s) you put together are highly personal and dependent on both your lifestyle and the threats you face.

Everyday ready (EDR) kits

That being said, there is a kit everyone should have: the everyday ready kit. This is a collection of items to help you deal with the kinds of everyday issues that can catch you off guard, or worse. In it should be those items that make life more pleasant and easier to deal with, as well as a few items to help you Respond to the kinds of moderate emergencies that are most likely to happen. This is the kit that's always with you, whether you're commuting, sitting in your office, or out on the town.

When you think about it, there are all kinds of events both large and small that could interrupt your normal routine, inconvenience you, or perhaps even threaten your health and safety. The impacts range from embarrassment to death, but it's possible to put together a small kit to help you get through them all.

Here's an example from my own life: Like many people, I've gone through the last decade-and-a-half dealing with the issues faced by my elderly parents and in-laws. It started when my Father, who died a few years ago, developed cancer then had a severe stroke. I spent many nights in hospitals, some of them quite a distance from home, with him. When my Mother's health began failing, late-night trips to the emergency room become normal. Between the two of them (and my wife's similarly aged parents), I've lived with the prospect of needing to drop whatever I'm doing (including sleeping) and head out at a moment's notice.

My EDR kit is my ever-present messenger bag. I started carrying one years ago to house my camera (my time as a commercial photographer left me with the habit of always having a camera present!). Today it still has a camera, but also a selection of items that make life a little easier when I'm called away from home unexpectedly. In the "health and beauty aids" department, I have antacids, snack bars, a stainless water bottle (which is always filled), a comb, toothbrush and toothpaste, lip balm, and a small tube of sunscreen.

It also contains a few tools I always seem to need, such as a compact multi-tool, a small but high-intensity flashlight, a small tape measure, tweezers and nail clippers, and a car charger for my phone. In that bag is also a trauma kit — because life-threatening injuries occur daily and everywhere. I firmly believe that a trauma kit, and the training necessary to use it, should be something everyone carries with them all the time.

An EDR kit may also include your self-defense tool(s) of choice. If, for instance, you regularly carry a defensive firearm, it's part of your EDR kit. I don't recommend carrying one in a messenger bag (I certainly don't), but it's still part of your kit.

There's more in my bag, but this should serve as an example of what to carry and why. My everyday ready kit allows me to maintain my comfort and composure in a hospital waiting room at 2 am, as well as helping me get through the first hours of a more severe emergency.

Your everyday ready kit might be in your briefcase or purse, or it may be a carefully chosen collection of items in your pockets. Whatever form your EDR kit is in, pick items to deal with the most likely emergencies, tasks, and inconveniences you'll face. You won't be able to carry enough to survive a week of a "grid-down" nightmare scenario, but you should carry enough to see you through to the next day.

Ask yourself, "What could plausibly happen right now to disrupt my life for the next 12 hours?" Think through all the implications, then stock your EDR kit to make your life easier should that happen.

"Bug Out" and "Bail Out" Bags (BOB)

BOBs are the staple of preparedness websites and books, and the inspiration for more "survival porn" than perhaps anything else. Everyone, it seems, has a BOB and just has to post pictures on Instagram about its contents!

I've already talked about the wisdom (or lack) of bugging out as a primary survival strategy, but the concept of the BOB is sound: to give you the items you need to get through a personal or widespread emergency if you're forced to leave your home. In my case, earthquakes are a very real threat and could render my house instantly uninhabitable. In such a case I might have to leave with only moments to take what I needed, which is the role fulfilled by the BOB.

The contents of your BOB will be partly determined by the kind of danger you feel would drive you from your home. A house fire is generally a personal emergency, and your BOB should contain things that allow you to get through a few hours until you find shelter, such as climate-appropriate clothing (in case you're forced directly out of bed and into the night), snacks, water, and enough money to get you into a hotel room.

If you're preparing for a more widespread emergency, one that forces you to leave the area on foot, your BOB might be more heavily weighted toward food, water, and shelter — resembling a backpacker's load for a long-distance hike.

Some people include a self-defense firearm in their BOB, though I'm not fond of this option. Storing a firearm in an emergency kit means the gun is largely unsecured, and I cannot condone that practice. If you feel the need for a self-defense firearm in an emergency, stage the gun in a way that allows you to retrieve it as you exit, but keeps it out of the hands of unauthorized people. This usually means some sort of quick-access safe or lockbox, or that you move the gun to a more secure safe when you're not around. Yes, it's a lot of work, but it's the only way to do so responsibly. A better strategy is to carry it on your person, where it's always available and always protected.

Get Home Bag (GHB)

The GHB is a specialized emergency kit and one I think more people need to consider. The get-home bag is a multi-hazard kit that gives you resources to facilitate making your way home if you're forced to abandon your vehicle.

This can happen due to any number of problems: You break down on a lonely stretch of road; a flood makes roads impassable; you slide off the road in inclement weather; violent protestors bring traffic to a standstill; or an earthquake collapses bridges. Whatever the cause, if you need to leave your car behind and get home (or to another place of safety), the GHB is what you'd take with you.

In the GHB you'd probably include inclement-weather clothing or protection, water and high-energy food, some way to purify water in case you're forced to take it from uncertain sources, maps and compass for navigating unfamiliar backroads or complex city streets, solar charger for your cell phone, and so on. Some folks include shelter, like a lightweight single-person tent. For many people, a sturdy and comfortable pair of walking shoes will be on top of the pile!

The GHB needs to be contained in a form that allows easy long-distance carry, such as. a backpack of some description, but be careful about the weight. It's easy to overload a pack to the point you can't carry it for more than a short distance.

Don't forget your medical needs, and include a first-aid kit with items to deal with injuries common to walking on rough terrain: blisters, scrapes, and cuts, and perhaps even broken finger bones from falling.

If you do any amount of commuting, always be prepared to walk home. The GHB makes it safer and less onerous.

The 72-hour kit

When faced with a serious disaster, the kind that threatens life and delays the arrival of rescue and relief assets, the 72-hour kit becomes the star of the show. The idea of the 72-hour kit is to allow you to remain completely independent for the first three full days of a disaster. The ideal 72-hour kit has sufficient food, water, shelter, sanitation supplies, and creature comforts to let you maintain life and minimize suffering until help arrives. It should also contain items to help you start the recovery and rebuilding process.

Hardcore survivalists insist that a 72-hour kit be able to be carried by an individual for long distances over rough terrain, but I don't believe it's a realistic goal. Instead, I encourage you to think of the 72-hour kit as something you can move around, but not necessarily sling on your back. Its purpose is to give you everything you need to support your health, well-being, and sanity in the first few days of a real emergency, and that's a lot of stuff to carry around!

The American Red Cross has long advocated keeping a 72-hour kit in your home and ready for use at a moment's notice. They suggest keeping your kit in easily moved plastic totes with covers, which makes a lot of sense.

Here are some ideas of what to include in your kit (everything is per person unless otherwise noted):

- Food sufficient for three full days (should not require much if any preparation or cooking)
- Clean water for three days (or a method to capture and purify water)
- Prescription medications
- Copies of your identification, bank account, and insurance documents (in case your originals are lost or destroyed)
- At least one change of clothing, and sufficient undergarments for the duration
- Hygiene supplies: soap (or better, no-rinse bath wipes), toothpaste, etc, and any items needed to use them
- Some form of communication to allow you to keep up on current events and official news (a solar-powered radio is perfect)
- Tools (knife, multi-tool, etc.)
- Sturdy shoes
- Outerwear suitable for the weather
- Entertainment and morale items (toys for the kids, reading material for the adults, and perhaps some snacks or drink mixes)
- Camp stove and fuel
- Serving utensils (plates, cups, forks, spoons, knives; make sure they're lightweight and durable. Plastic may be best.)
- Tent(s) (and perhaps some method to heat them if you live in a very cold climate)
- Sleeping bags and mats

As you see, it's a pretty extensive list. Only an experienced backpacker in good shape can carry that much gear around for any length of time. I'll admit I couldn't, and I'll wager most Americans couldn't either. Accept the realities of your age and health, and build a comprehensive kit that addresses your needs rather than making concessions to portability. If you do need to leave your home, that's what your BOB is for.

Think through the kinds of disaster scenarios where the 72-hour kit might be vital to your survival, and then place your kit where it will be accessible in the aftermath. For instance, keeping the kit in a back corner of your garage might make it impossible to access after an earthquake or tornado. It would be better to keep it near an opening (door or window) through which you can retrieve it.

Which kit do you build first?

Start with your everyday ready (EDR) kit. Think about the things you might carry with you that would help, even in a small way, you be more prepared for both normal life and an abnormal event. If you don't carry a pocket knife, start doing so. A knife is mankind's basic tool, usable for myriad tasks from opening packages to cutting through seatbelts to rescue someone. I've carried a pocket knife every single day since I was in the third or fourth grade (of course, I'm old enough that schools allowed such things!). It's one of two items I'm never without.

I consider a small, high-intensity flashlight a "must" for everyday carry. As a safety and defense tool, it's usable over an unusually wide range of circumstances, from spotting threats far away to distracting a possible attacker to being used as an impact weapon. In addition, it's useful when the power goes out and your workplace is suddenly dark. And you'd be surprised how handy it is for looking in the corners of a supply closet or even the recesses of your car's trunk! I use my flashlight multiple times every single day, and have twice used it against criminals to de-escalate what could have become nasty incidents.

There are many other things that I carry and you could, but your EDR kit needs to fit your life. Think consciously and logically about what you could always have on your person to enhance your safety, comfort, and survival. Then figure out a way to keep those things on or very near your body, either in your pockets, briefcase, backpack, purse, or some combination of those. The EDR kit doesn't need to be a kit, in the sense that it's kept together in one spot, but it does need to be with you in some form.

If you choose to carry a firearm, consider it part of your EDR kit.

Don't forget the medical kit!

In another chapter, I talk about the medical emergency and dealing with severe trauma, but remember the medical kit is first and foremost an emergency kit. But unlike your other kits, it's one you need training to use properly. While you're building your emergency kits, think about medical Response. If you haven't yet gotten trauma casualty care training, make that part of your emergency kit plans. Once you've gotten a trauma course under your belt, add medical kits to your inventory of emergency supplies.

I carry a trauma kit with me wherever I go — including on an airliner. If I'm going somewhere that I can't take my full kit, I have a smaller version that fits into a suit-coat pocket without being too noticeable. I'm currently experimenting with such a kit carried on my ankle*, and it's quite concealable. (I know one person who attended a black-tie event with this very kit on his leg! No one noticed.)

Your kits will change over time

Don't expect the contents of any of your kits to remain static. The more personal the kit, the more (and more often) you can expect it to change. You'll develop new skills or better identify what you need to Respond to various kinds of incidents. Your wardrobe or job may change, or you may find more comfortable ways of keeping safety and survival gear with you. Of course, as mentioned above, your kids will change and their kits will too.

Commit yourself to periodically revisiting all your kits, thinking carefully about the contents and how they fit into your life. Anytime something in your life changes, consider how that affects your preparedness and by extension your preparedness kits. Make changes as appropriate.

Maintaining your emergency kits

Like so many other parts of your preparedness life, your emergency kits need to be maintained. Some of the items in your kits, such as food and medicines, have expiration dates and need to be replaced. Other items may need maintenance, such as batteries or items powered by batteries. Establish a regular schedule to rotate or replace those things as necessary, especially if they're subject to environmental extremes (such as being stored in your car). Enter the frequency of scheduled inspection or rotation into your matrix form.

A good example is your trauma response kit. I recommend everyone carry a trauma kit with tourniquets and hemostatic (blood clotting) agents, and of course have the training to use them properly. Most hemostatic products have an expiration date, and it's a really good idea to replace them when they expire to maintain their performance. When it comes to food, expiration dates aren't that important, but I tend to be much more conservative with items I expect to save lives.

Watch for wear and tear

You may find that some items in your kits sustain wear and tear simply being carried around regularly. The trauma kit I carry with me daily sees a lot of wear, and every so often the packaging on one of the sterile items wears through. I've had it happen to hemostatic gauze, necessitating its replacement.

Plan to physically inspect each of your kits on a consistent basis, and replace any item you're unsure about. The more often you carry it around or the harsher the environment in which it's stored, the more often you need to check it. Be sure to update your Matrix form with the next inspection date so you have a reminder.

* — SFD Responder: www.saferfasterdefense.com/product/sfd-responder/

JOB LOSS

It might seem odd to talk about job or income loss in a book about personal security. After all, we've been talking about how to protect and save your life from various kinds of disasters, about protection strategies and self-defense. Compared to those, a job loss doesn't seem to fit the theme of this book.

In reality, though, a job loss may be the most common crisis most people face in their lives. For many people, it will happen more than once, and it can be devastating, significantly affecting their life for years and perhaps even posing a threat to their health and well-being.

Like all the other things we've talked about, it's also something for which you can prepare.

It's true that the loss of a job in and of itself isn't immediately life-threatening, at least for most people. Our social safety net has been constructed to support displaced workers for short periods of time so they can find new employment. During that period, lifestyles may need to be adjusted, but the basic needs of the person (and his or her family) are at least nominally provided.

But what if you can't find a job before those benefits run out?

"It can't happen to me"

The world is changing more rapidly with each passing day. Automation, which first displaced blue-collar workers on assembly lines, is now taking its toll on white- collar jobs as well. Jobs that required a human's thought and ingenuity are now being done by computers. Accountants and attorneys are now in the sights of computer systems armed with huge amounts of data and algorithms that enable them to make decisions once considered the domain of humans alone.

Even jobs I would have said couldn't be automated — like driving a truck — are at this very moment being done on an experimental basis by technology. It's easy to think we're important, unique, and irreplaceable, but the truth is very different. Many people who once believed themselves to be immune from the vicissitudes of the employment marketplace are today finding themselves without incomes.

If you've never been faced with the prospect of long-term unemployment, you're rapidly becoming a minority. The chances are quite good that, in the next decade, you'll see your job affected by the relentless march of technology. And this assumes an overall good economy. If we enter a recession, it'll happen sooner. Machines are cheaper than people, and they don't complain or require expensive benefits.

The worst part? No one, except you, will seem to care.

The risks of long-term unemployment

The government defines long-term unemployment as job loss lasting 27 weeks or more, or roughly six months. That's a long time to be without income. It's also a long time to be without the emotional benefits of having a job.

For many people, their job defines who they are. It's their identity. When their identity is taken away, they can suffer psychological, emotional, and even physical illness. It's not unusual for someone facing joblessness of months or even years to suffer depression, anger, and stress. These can result in cardiovascular problems, family breakups, emotional or physical abuse, or self-harm. It can even lead to long-term changes in personality traits.

Are you beginning to sense why I included unemployment as a risk to prepare for?

Preparedness isn't just for tornadoes and hurricanes

First, given the increasing likelihood of a job loss at some point in your career, and its devastating effects, you should consider preparing for it just as you prepare for the physical risks you've identified.

Part of your preparations should include setting aside a small amount of money every paycheck for what used to be called a "rainy-day fund." This is money to be used only for emergencies (and, frankly, it's a good idea for any sort of disaster).

Deciding ahead of time what you'll do when faced with a job loss can be a big motivator. If you decide you'll take any job that comes along, whether or not it's in your field or even if it's "beneath" your former occupation, it's easier to do when you need to. Like any preparedness activity, making a decision ahead of time reduces the anxiety when you're confronted with it. It's like preplanning your Responses as part of self-defense training: All you need is the trigger event to smoothly implement your Response plan.

On a more practical note, having a stock of food on hand (which is something you should do as part of your preparations for a widespread disaster) can be quite a comfort during periods of lower income. Knowing where your next meal is coming from reduces a surprising amount of anxiety about the future. Having the knowledge, skills, and supplies to deal with minor medical emergencies is likewise a confidence booster when you can't run to the doctor for every little injury. (This is a big advantage even if you're not faced with a job loss!)

One of the things experts suggest for maintaining your emotional and psychological well-being during unemployment is to stay busy. Aside from job hunting, you'll find yourself with many hours every week that used to be filled with commuting and working. Channel some of those hours into your preparedness planning. I've found keeping an eye on the future and thinking long term is a great way to get past the depression of the present and keep my mind active.

Finally, if you've taken my previous advice and gotten to know your neighbors and others whom you expect to come together during a widespread emergency, you'll find a ready-made support network. One common prescription for dealing with job loss is to maintain personal relationships, and your circle of like-minded neighbors and friends will see a job loss as a survival incident. You might be surprised who in your circle knows someone who is looking for just the skills you have. At the very least, you have someone to talk with who can listen and provide unbiased perspective on your plight.

References:

www.everydayhealth.com/emotional-health/effects-of-long-term-unemployment.aspx

www.empowher.com/mental-health/content/mental-physical-health-effects-long-term-unemployment

mentalhealthdaily.com/2015/02/25/long-term-unemployment-changes-personality-traits/

www.theweek.com/articles/450415/mental-anguish-longterm-unemployed

www.motherjones.com/kevin-drum/2013/12/10-reasons-long-term-unemployment-national-catastrophe

www.theatlantic.com/business/archive/2014/06/the-mental-health-consequences-of-unemployment/372449/

THE END OF THE WORLD AS WE KNOW IT

A few years ago, a reality television show called *Doomsday Preppers* showcased people who were, to be charitable, on the fringes of the preparedness world. They were hoarding all manner of food and sundries in preparation for the collapse of society — or, in hardcore prepper terms, TEOTWAWKI: The End Of The World As We Know It.

While the show was a ratings success for National Geographic, on whose network it aired, it convinced a lot of people that preparedness was an activity for the mentally unhinged. As you make your own life more resilient to disruption, you might be tempted to ask: Should I be concerned about TEOTWAWKI?

What is this odd term?

TEOTWAWKI stems from the notion that a cataclysmic event could so alter the fabric of our society that the basic necessities of life would become scarce or non-existent. Infrastructure would be destroyed or rendered inoperable, and even the most basic services would cease.

At the same time, proponents believe, cultural changes would be so profound that societal norms would disappear or be altered to a significant degree. Depending on whose version of the narrative you listen to, government would either disappear entirely (anarchism) or be taken over by despotic rulers who would enslave the population (dystopianism). People would turn on each other, neighbors would become lethal enemies, and heavily armed bands of looters would rule the countryside.

In short, the post-event world they foresee would be completely different in every way than the world we live in today. Hence, The End Of The World As We Know It (now).

This state could, in their view, be brought about by any number of things: a pandemic, perhaps as part of a biological terror attack, which kills off enough people to affect government stability; a nuclear exchange among the major world powers; a rogue nation-state exploding a nuclear warhead above the country, resulting in an EMP blast that damages all our electronics; a terrorist attack using a dirty bomb, setting off a chain reaction of government over-reach and enslaving the populace; a massive solar flare that results in EMP damage (EMP is very big with the doomsday crowd); and for the religiously motivated, the Second Coming, Rapture, and probably a number of supernatural events I'm not schooled on.

Is this something you should worry about? More importantly, is it something you should consider when doing your Response planning?

What's really likely?

Let's go back to our discussion of the States of Expectation. All the trigger events the TEOTWAWKI true believers see happening have varying levels of plausibility. A pandemic (whether natural or manmade) is a real possibility. They've certainly happened in the past, and while modern medicine has reduced their risk, we're learning that drug-resistant bugs pop up in the wild with some regularity. Is it possible that such a bug could evolve (either naturally or with help) to be both virulent and easily transmitted? Certainly. It's even possible that, with rapid air travel now commonplace nearly everywhere in the world, it could spread to major population centers even before being detected and identified.

So it's possible. But is it likely? That depends on your assessment and level of knowledge about epidemiology, but I'd say not very. Is it plausible, then? In my estimation, yes. However, that's a long way from TEOTWAWKI!

The trigger event might be plausible or even likely. For a true end of society to occur, though, requires more than just a trigger. It requires a chain of decisions and actions that result in widespread destruction of life or property (or both). If you apply the States of Expectation analysis to each link in that chain, I think you'll come to the conclusion that the horrific results attributed to any given trigger are quite unlikely and generally implausible. Possible? Yes, but remember our definition of possible is "limited only by the laws of physics." Lots of things are possible, in the sense that those laws don't prevent them, but they carry little to no degree of likelihood.

Is a nuclear exchange among superpowers possible? Of course it is, and we've come uncomfortably close to one several times since the dawn of the atomic age. Is it likely or plausible? You can decide that for yourself. A massive solar flare? Certainly plausible and perhaps even likely (it's happened in my lifetime, and a history of observed solar flares goes back more than a century). I could go on, but the point is that any of these trigger events might happen. But the event aftermath these people prepare for is less likely.

The End Of Your World As You Know It

I think it's far more prudent to prepare for things that could plausibly and irretrievably alter **your** life, because those things happen every day all across our nation. This whole book, in fact, is about avoiding The End Of Your World As You Know It, At Least For A Little While (TEOYWAYKIALFALW): events that so radically change your life

that you are unable to resume it immediately, and that hold the potential for longer-term disruption.

These events happen constantly. Think of all the plausible threats you
identified as part of the Anticipate function and assigned their own
matrix. How many of them would affect your ability to go to work, or
where you'll sleep tonight, or even how much money you have left? It's
likely all of them have the potential to do all of those things, at least in
the short term.

Take the common house fire. Imagine everything you own, everything
you hold dear, wiped off the face of the earth. Yes, insurance would
help you rebuild, but your life would change drastically. In the long run
it might actually improve. I've talked to many people who regarded it
as a positive fresh start, but it took them years to get to that realization. In the short term, they all felt as though their lives had been
destroyed, because they had.

I believe the key is to be able to see past your immediate problems and
look to the future and the end of the incident. This is where your planning and preparation are your biggest assets; by being prepared to
weather the storm, you'll be able to see the sun beyond the dark
clouds. You'll also have the means to survive long enough to see it. You
live for the Recovery.

It's not just survival, either. Your preparations give you the resiliency
you need to Recover with the least amount of disruption possible. If
the life-altering event is a self-defense incident, your training and
knowledge in the use of force may likely keep you from being
convicted of a crime yourself. You'll be able to proceed through the
justice system with as little disruption as possible.

If the event is a car wreck in which a member of your family is criti-
cally injured, your preparations for dealing with life-threatening
trauma may make the difference between a funeral and a relatively
short stay in the ICU followed by a complete recovery.

The matrix forms you've been filling out in the Anticipate stage are
really forecasts of TEOYWAYKIALFALW. When you look at them,

do they paint a realistic picture of what is plausible in your life? Consider them together, as a whole: Is the picture you see reasonable, or have you concocted a Hollywood fantasy?

Focusing on the threats that might be the end of YOUR world as YOU know it, as opposed to the dystopian *Mad Max* fantasies of preppers gone over the edge, is how you develop resiliency. These are your threats, your risks, and your plans to survive them. They'll help you live your life and hopefully let you resume it as soon as possible.

Isn't that why you're reading this book?

RECOVERY

Have you ever watched a movie or television program where the hero is severely injured, and at the end he or she appears in perfect shape, having made a miraculously rapid recovery? Ever thought how silly that was, knowing even with advanced medical treatment they'd be looking at weeks in the hospital and months in physical therapy just to walk again?

That kind of fantasy infects our preparedness planning too. Almost everyone I've met and virtually all the students I've talked with have an unrealistic view about the aftermath of a self-defense incident, disaster, or medical emergency. It never occurs to them that the legal, physical, psychological, and financial impacts of life-altering events are significant, let alone something they need to plan for.

One reason for adopting the Adaptive Personal Security approach, though, is to minimize disruption to your life. Understanding the kinds of threats you face, and the ways in which you can Deter them, Detect them in advance of their arrival, and Respond efficiently if necessary, is how you do it. Dealing with the aftermath, the effects of which can be worse than the event itself, is part of minimizing disruptions. Recovery is part and parcel of your Response, and therefore needs to be part of your Anticipation planning as well.

What is Recovery?

Recovery refers to all the things that happen after the specific threat has passed. Think of Recovery as dealing with the side effects of an event: The threat itself has gone, but what it has left in its wake is still affecting your life and/or health. The aftermath of an incident may have both immediate and long-term ramifications, and by paying attention to Recovery, you minimize their impact on you and the people around you.

Recovery may start seconds after the incident has ended and may continue for months, maybe even years. It may involve immediate medical care for injuries you or others have sustained, dealing with law enforcement and the justice system, documentation of loss for insurance, and counseling for the very often ignored effects of PTSD. All of these, and many more, are in the province of Recovery.

Recovery suggests prevention

For any given threat, there may be more than one Response, more than one course of action that will result in your survival and safety. For any one of those courses of action, there may be many things you must contend with in the Recovery process. Sometimes the Recovery process suggests better ways to Respond or emphasizes the need for better Deterrence and Detection.

Many people who haven't put together the kind of comprehensive security plan you have may buy a gun and believe they're "ready for anything." They don't get proper training in how to use it efficiently or, more importantly, when the use of lethal force is justifiable. When, in the middle of the night, they're surprised by their front doorknob rattling, their only Response option is the gun, which they fire through the door, killing the innocent neighbor on the other side. I'm aware of two news stories within the last year where similar scenarios played out.

Recovery from such an outcome will be long, stressful, and likely very expensive. The person may be indicted and forced to defend himself through a criminal trial. If he's found criminally negligent, he'll spend time in prison. His life will be destroyed. Even if found not guilty, a civil suit from the family members of the person who was killed may prove unimaginably costly. (The burden of proof in a civil trial is much less than in a criminal trial, and it's not unheard of for a defendant to win the latter and lose the former.) In any case, the homeowner will no doubt have emotional and psychological issues the rest of his life, perhaps severe enough to require hospitalization.

On the other hand, considering Recovery as part of the planning process might suggest a different approach to the problem. If the homeowner takes a rational look at the threat of burglary while the home is occupied, instead of his first step being to buy a gun, he might decide to start with better lighting. A way of identifying people at the door without exposing himself to the threat would be indicated, along with hardening the door and locks to substantially delay intrusion. Establishing a safe room — probably the master bedroom — with a solid lockable door and a cell phone on a charger further isolates the occupants from the threat and allows them to call for law enforcement response. Then a firearm can be added for the worst-case scenario of the burglar actually making it through all those Deter and Detect measures.

Now let's say the same scenario occurs with someone who has prepared this way: The homeowner sees on his computer screen that the person jiggling the doorknob is in fact a drunken neighbor who has mistaken their house for his, and instead of shooting blindly through the door, the homeowner invites the neighbor in, sets him down on the couch, and calls the neighbor's wife to come pick him up. Recovery in this case involves making coffee.

The ramifications of anything you do, and the side effects of any of your Response options, should be considered ahead of time. Recovery from the use of deadly force will always be significant and entails considerable risks no matter how justified it may be. Factoring Recovery into your Anticipation planning is key to minimizing the ultimate impact of any threat you face.

In the next several chapters we'll take a closer look at the legal, financial, and psychological aspects of Recovery.

LEGAL RECOVERY

The threats you've identified likely include criminal actions: carjack-ings, muggings, home invasions, and so on. Responding to threats from the criminal activities of other humans usually requires some sort of physical Response, which may be in the form of a weapon, ranging from a baseball bat to a knife to a firearm. Whenever you use a weapon to defend yourself and end up doing physical damage to another human being, there will be legal ramifications. (Even if you point a gun at someone without shooting them, there are likely to be legal issues!)

This is such an important point I'll make it again: If you use a weapon — any sort of weapon — to defend yourself, there will be legal ramifi-cations that take time and very often lots of money to resolve. I point this out not to force you into submission because you fear the possible legal aftermath of defending yourself, but to establish the fact that you need to be prepared to legally Recover from your use of force.

If your use of force against an attacker is clearly appropriate, the legal ramifications will likely be minimal and relatively easily dealt with. This doesn't mean they won't be non-existent or trivial, only easy to handle compared to the alternative. The problem is many incidents are far from cut and dried, relying as they do on your judgement of the risk to your life (or the lives of others). They also involve others' interpretations of what you did and whether they think it was appropriate.

Ultimately, the only way to find out if your actions were appropriate under the law is to go through the criminal justice system, which brings with it the possibility that others won't see you as the white knight.

Recovery in the legal sense means understanding the legal system and how you might be judged, then navigating your way to exoneration. Be very clear, however: It's not always easy, and almost never cheap!

What happens after you've defended yourself?

If you've used a weapon or injured anyone (yes, even your attacker), be prepared to be arrested. This isn't a reflection on your guilt or innocence, but simply the normal course of action when police find someone injured or killed by another. Your arrest is part of their investigation, and may last only a short time if it becomes clear that you were in fact the victim.

Your weapon, regardless of what it is, will likely be seized for the duration of the investigation and any legal proceedings. Your favorite gun may sit in an evidence locker for months or even years.

Depending on the jurisdiction, the police will present the evidence they've gathered to the public prosecutor (usually a District Attorney), who will look at the case and decide whether to indict you with a crime. In other jurisdictions, the DA presents the case to a Grand Jury, who determine whether the evidence warrants a trial. In my observations, most clearly legitimate self-defense cases end at this stage, with the DA unwilling to prosecute or the Grand Jury returning a decision of "no true bill."

But that's not always the case, and some authorities in the self-defense community maintain a DA who has political aspirations or is up for re-election may prosecute indiscriminately. Some District Attorneys, they point out, are notoriously anti-gun and try to prosecute any case involving a firearm, including legitimate self-defense. While I believe them to be few and far between, a friend of mine faced such a DA recently — despite not actually using his gun to defend himself and a friend from a violent truck driver! The mere fact he had a gun with him was enough for the DA to attempt an indictment, until incontrovertible video evidence was recovered.

If you are indicted with a crime, you'll proceed to a criminal trial. You may spend a couple of years and several hundreds of thousands of dollars to defend yourself. As I mentioned earlier, even if you win, in many states the victim's family can sue you in civil court. The civil case may happen though the DA or Grand Jury declines to indict you.

Again, I am not trying to scare you into submission when faced with a criminal assault. But if you have a firearm for self-defense, you need to understand that using it will put you into the criminal justice system at some point, and things may take time to get resolved. Be prepared to Recover from such an ordeal before it happens!

The Recovery plan

Become knowledgeable about the laws regarding self-defense: You don't need to become a lawyer to understand the criminal justice system and how it handles self-defense claims, but you do need a lawyer to explain it. Again, I recommend the book *The Law of Self Defense* by attorney Andrew Branca for its complete and readable treatment of a confusing topic.

Mitchell Lake, Associate Attorney at Rachel M. Baird & Associate in Harwinton, Connecticut, has a very good way of explaining things: "Your job as a lawfully armed person is to not make the police or prosecution have to go forward with prosecuting the case because they have questions about the propriety of the actions you have taken." Knowing the law ahead of time will help you do that!

Learn how to interact with police after an incident: Learning how to deal with the police who respond and investigate your case is critical to a successful outcome. Many people espouse the belief that you should "clam up" when the police arrive and let your lawyer do the talking later, but doing so might mean police miss witnesses and evidence that could establish your innocence. Massad Ayoob's excellent MAG-20 curriculum*, mentioned earlier, is the best place to learn how and why you should interact with the police who arrive on scene — and the investigators who will follow.

The special case of self-defense insurance

In recent years, a number of self-defense insurance programs have been offered from a variety of start-up companies. Their aim is to help you through the legal aspects of defending your actions in court, which is a stunningly expensive activity. Only a severe protracted illness, such as cancer, has the potential to do as much financial damage.

If you're charged criminally, your legal defense could easily run into hundreds of thousands of dollars. If you're unlucky enough to face an additional civil suit from the family of a criminal who was injured or killed through your defensive actions, you'll likely spend double that (and then some).

The risk would seem to make a good case for having self-defense insurance in place, but is that really prudent? Like self-defense planning, it comes down to your assessment of the risk and the likelihood.

What are the risks?

First, consider how likely it is that you'll be involved in a self-defense incident where another person is hurt or killed by your defensive actions. While the risk of criminal attack is declining overall, many people each year still face a violent crime. This is why we prepare by learning how to defend ourselves.

How many of those cases end up in court? That's hard to say, and I'm not aware of any reliable statistics on the matter. But it's reasonable to say that legitimate cases of self-defense, where the good guy was a law-abiding, upstanding citizen, are not usually prosecuted. Still, some do end up in court and the fees mount substantially.

It's not a "clean" shooting until someone says it is

Many people believe in some simplistic view of self-defense where, if your actions in the moment are "justified," no legal harm can befall you. It's not that simple. Even in the most clear-cut self-defense incidents, there are almost always small details that, if looked at from a particular viewpoint, might seem shady.

Your actions aren't justified until judged so by someone else, and that judgement is based on the entirety of your incident. Whether by a judge and jury, or a District Attorney who declines to prosecute, someone else decides if your actions were appropriate under the circumstances.

That process might likely cost you a lot of money, even before you're actually charged. Attorneys start billing from the moment they're retained, for instance. If there are details that need interpretation the costs go up. Your own perception of your innocence is immaterial to defending yourself in court; it's about the evidence.

Even if your self-defense actions in and of themselves are justifiable, you may have committed other crimes in the process. Some jurisdictions have magazine capacity limitations; if you use a banned magazine to shoot an intruder, even if the shooting was appropriate, you might be prosecuted for the magazine violation.

Similar things have been known to happen with regard to ordinances against discharging firearms inside city limits. If you're carrying a defensive firearm without the appropriate licenses, don't expect that detail to be ignored by the authorities merely because you were justified in shooting your attacker.

It's worth noting most (if not all) of the self-defense insurance programs do not cover associated illegal acts. In other words, if you violate an ordinance while using your ordnance, don't expect your insurance to cover you.

Malicious prosecution

There are also those thankfully rare cases where otherwise innocent, law-abiding citizens have been prosecuted for using force against an attacker. A politically ambitious prosecutor, keen to be elected to office (or facing re-election), has on rare occasion prosecuted someone for a self-defense action to further their own career. Remember those little inconsistencies I spoke of earlier? An ambitious prosecutor may seize upon these in an attempt to convict you.

Again, I believe these cases to be uncommon, but I do have one friend who faced prosecution for an alleged case of assault with a deadly weapon. The other person involved in the incident claimed my friend — a firearms instructor and radio host of a self-defense show — threatened him with a gun. It was one man's word against the other, and the prosecutor took the case on because of a personal bias against firearms ownership. Luckily the entire interaction was caught on surveillance cameras from multiple angles and, after several hearings, the prosecutor finally dropped the case. It still cost my friend nearly $20,000 in legal fees, however.

As I said, malicious prosecution is rare. But it does happen.

Preventing legal challenges

Barring the unreasonable prosecution, most of the incidents I've reviewed over the years ended up in court because of a lack of knowledge on the part of the defender (later defendant). Not knowing when the use of lethal force is warranted often results in legal issues. Using a firearm to defend property is the most common transgression, as in the case of the person who responds to a car prowl with a gun. In just the last year, I've read of at least a dozen such cases!

Pursuing criminals is another common mistake too many people make.

Firing warning shots when lethal force is not justified is another, and intervening in someone else's incident is unfortunately often a recipe for disaster. As this is being written, in a news story out of North Carolina, a man intervened in a struggle when two employees of a mental-health facility were trying to restrain a patient who'd gotten away from them on a supervised outing. The man not only pulled his gun but fired a warning shot! His defense? "I've been told if I saw anything going on, I could use lethal force."

I discuss the financial implications of self-defense insurance in the next chapter.

* — *Massad Ayoob's "Armed Citizen's Rules of Engagement" course: www.massadayoobgroup.com/mag-20-classroom/*

FINANCIAL RECOVERY

People don't typically think of the financial costs of Recovery from an incident, but your financial condition is something you need to consider. An event that threatens your life may leave you vulnerable to financial catastrophe, which can affect you for as long as you live. At the same time, this is an area where it's very easy to spend more money than necessary. Financial decisions, including protecting your finances, need to be made carefully. I've seen cases where people had become so fearful of protecting their assets that they spent ridiculous amounts of money on insurance policies they didn't need.

I hate to keep repeating this, but it really does come down to balance — and each individual's balance is different.

Financial recovery planning often serves as a check to your other planning. In my own case, considering the financial effects of a particular threat sometimes changed how I approached prevention and Response. Those changes usually made me safer and at the same time reduced my financial exposure. This underscores the value of the whole-systems approach of Adaptive Personal Security. I like to think of it as holistic personal safety!

Thinking about financial recovery

When you think about financial recovery, what's the first word that pops into your head? If you're like most people, the word is "insurance," which exists to make you whole (or as close to it as possible) after a loss. In many life-altering incidents, you'll experience financial losses. Whether it's a car accident, critical injury on the job, debilitating illness, or death of a spouse or partner, insurance steps in to cover those financial losses.

In preparing for Recovery, have a look at your insurance. Ask yourself if you need coverage for the losses you might incur as a result of the items on your threat list. For instance, massive floods happen all over the country every year, and many people live in places where such catastrophes are of the "when, not if" variety. An insurance agent once told me that perhaps only a quarter of people who live in flood plains have any sort of flood insurance, because it's not part of most homeowner's insurance plans. It must be purchased separately, and apparently few do.

I'm not saying you need to go out and buy flood insurance. I am saying you need to look at your own situation and ask if the money you might spend on that kind of insurance is reasonable for you. If it's not, perhaps you shouldn't buy it.

The same goes for any sort of insurance for any sort of loss. Look at your identified threats, consider what a financial loss might be, and then consider whether it's worth insuring against. You might decide, even though the event is relatively high on the incidence scale, your potential losses have been reduced through your Deter, Detect, and Respond planning and don't warrant an insurance expense.

Other approaches to financial protection

Beyond insurance, what else might you do to secure financial recovery after an incident? You can make arrangements to avoid having a financial loss in the first place! As you work through your Deter worksheets, think in terms of what you can do at each stage to help your financial recovery. Many of the prevention steps I've talked about can help forestall a financial setback. If you can do something that both reduces the chances of an incident and at the same time reduces the financial effects if it happens, you should probably do it.

Think also in terms of your personal financial resilience. In today's economy, things change rapidly, and what you once thought was a stable position can suddenly disappear as the company reorganizes or is purchased and moved. In just the last year, almost a dozen people I know have faced exactly this scenario, including my wife! Some suffered severe financial setbacks.

You might prepare for a career setback by working on what's known as a "side gig": a money-generating activity you enjoy doing and that can be rapidly "spun up" if necessary to help you weather a financial storm. Many people discover that not only do they enjoy their side gig more than their day job, they can actually make more money at it and end up switching careers. Seeing to your financial recovery could, in fact, improve your life by reducing your stress and increasing your happiness.

Choosing a self-defense insurance plan

Today a number of companies offer some sort of self-defense insurance. Though not all of them are technically insurance, they all serve the same purpose. The concept is to provide you with the funds you need to retain a lawyer and see your case through the court system. Like any insurance, you should weigh the cost against the likelihood of need to determine if it's right for you.

If you decide in the affirmative, consider the following:

- The program needs to pay you up front. Some self-defense insurance pays off only after you've been acquitted, which means you need to finance hundreds of thousands of dollars yourself. Just retaining an attorney usually means writing a check for thousands of dollars. If you can't absorb those costs yourself, you won't get proper representation and your insurance program may be useless.

- The program should pay out regardless of the ultimate verdict. The reason to have self-defense insurance is so you can defend yourself in court. If the program stipulates that you must be acquitted of the charges before you get paid, it hasn't served the purpose of giving you the funds to defend yourself.
- The program should have defined and guaranteed benefits. You need to know what to expect, exactly what you'll get, and exactly when you'll get it. Some programs require a review of your case before any payout, and you may be subject to decisions over which you have no appeal. Make sure you know what your program will do for you and get it in writing.
- The program should have a track record. Many companies are entering this market, probably because it's very profitable. Some of them are brand new and have no experience in dealing with self-defense cases. A company that has been around some years and has dealt with more than a handful of cases gives you a base of expectation and a yardstick by which you can judge their performance.

I believe you should consider the relative rarity of prosecution of self-defense incidents and educate yourself about the nuances of self-defense law. You may still feel that self-defense insurance is important to you, and if so, I offer the following guidance.

The first approach is a true insurance policy, where an insurance company underwrites the policy. Most insurance policies, though not all, suffer from one particular weakness: you must have a loss (i.e., have paid an attorney to defend you) before they'll pay off. Good attorneys almost always require large retainers up front just to represent you, and that money comes out of your pocket. What's more, under many policies, you're reimbursed only if you win your case. If you are convicted or accept a plea deal, they often won't cover you.

On the plus side, insurance benefits are contractually guaranteed. As long as you meet the terms of the insurance contract, which are stated up front, you'll get paid.

The other approach is a membership organization, where the dues to belong are pooled into a defense fund. These programs can be more flexible, generally promising to provide money up front to retain an attorney. Most self-defense cases, like my friend's, are resolved without going to trial, and the money provided up front is often all that's needed. They provide coverage for the most likely scenario without out-of-pocket expense. Beyond that, they usually promise to provide money to mount an actual defense in court, should the case make it that far — and should it pass some sort of internal test as to the validity of your case. The amount is often variable and based on the need of the member.

The downside of membership organizations is that they may not be contractually obligated to provide any specific service. In those cases, you're relying on their integrity to fulfill their promises. Because their management is responsible for the funds entrusted to their care, and those funds have a finite limit, they're forced to review cases before committing members' resources. The criteria for such review may not be transparent, which again means you're relying on their integrity.

In essence, if you have an incident, you need to apply for coverage, and that coverage may be denied without recourse. Also, because their financial underpinnings are limited to what their members have provided through their dues, a run of cases could deplete their funds and leave others with no coverage. That's never happened, to the best of my knowledge, and it's a very unlikely scenario, but it is possible.

Each approach has its advantages and disadvantages, and programs change frequently. If you're considering a self-defense insurance plan, read the benefits and limitations carefully before spending your money.

PSYCHOLOGICAL RECOVERY

A good friend's mother spent many years as a counselor, specifically dealing with people who had survived traumatic incidents. She had no office, at least not a consistent one — she was on a disaster response team for the American Red Cross, and her bags were literally always packed for activation at a moment's notice. The Red Cross understood the importance of psychological intervention in the immediate aftermath of any disaster, and a big part of their response was sending counselors like her directly into the disaster area, sometimes for a month at a time, to help survivors through the difficult times they faced.

Aside from their lack of general preparedness, she said most people weren't ready for the psychological trauma of losing their homes (or loved ones) in a disaster. For many, the mental anguish was far worse than the physical loss and often persisted for months or even years after the event.

Part of your Response planning needs to be an understanding of how an incident can affect you psychologically and emotionally. Human beings are social animals. With the exception of the occasional hermit, we want to be around others. That desire may be tempered with the realization that certain others are more trouble than they're worth, and that we can only deal with others in controlled increments, but we all need someone, sometime.

Any incident that requires your Response to survive carries with it some social changes. The degree and type of those changes depend on the incident, how you handle it, and sometimes how you prepare ahead of time.

Shared misery

In a widespread disaster event, where your neighbors may be affected as much (or even more) than you are, social cohesion is often affected. While it's easy to dwell on the horror stories of human depravity after an event, such as reports of vicious looters in the aftermath of storms and earthquakes, in many other instances, communities have shown a tendency to pull together. This shared misery often has positive outcomes, with neighbors becoming closer and communities seeing a surge of spirit and cooperation.

Unfortunately, even in cases where that's true, it may only be temporary. A community may be irretrievably damaged, to the point that it ceases to exist in its old form. New Orleans after Hurricane Katrina is a good example: Entire neighborhoods were wiped out, their occupants unable or unwilling to rebuild. The condemned houses were eventually bulldozed, leaving many blocks with only a few — or no — residents.

What my research suggests, however, is the closer communities were before the event, the more likely they are to survive through Recovery largely intact. There truly is no substitute for knowing your neighbors!

Getting closer

It seems, then, moving to a tight-knit community (or working to develop community cohesion where you live) is a valuable asset to Recovery. Having grown up and lived in rural communities, where people help one another as a matter of course, this seems natural to me. More than once I've been the recipient of much-needed assistance from my neighbors, and more than once I've given that help. This cooperative spirit has made severe winter storms easier to bear and helped fight a fast-moving fire that threatened to destroy our barn. I have no doubt that in a widespread incident, where many people are affected, the same community spirit would greatly aid both survival of the incident itself and the Recovery from it.

Preventing conflict

This kind of community cohesion has benefits that extend beyond Response and Recovery. Knowing you might need to rely on the people around you, and they on you, has an effect on interpersonal conflict. Growing up in a farming and logging community taught me this at an early age. I knew my Father wasn't fond of certain people, but he made it a point to get along with them because it was important to the strength of our small community. As an adult I do the same thing, for the same reasons. I might need them someday, and I want to return the favor, so I make it a point to get along with my neighbors despite any differences of opinion we might have.

(This is, admittedly, made easier by having neighbors who are easy to get along with, but it's also a matter of luck — and could change tomorrow if someone new moved in.)

Watching out for each other

Communities that get along also tend to watch out for each other. The basis of Neighborhood Watch programs is, after all, neighbors watching out for each other.

When you know your neighbors and get along with them, there is a motivation to make sure nothing bad happens to them. Keeping watch so no one breaks into their house is one way to look out for your neighbors. Early one morning, I spotted a dangerous chimney fire at my neighbor's house and woke them in time to prevent loss of both property and life. A neighbor once sought our help because of an abusive episode with her spouse, because she felt we would look out for her (she was right, both during and after the event).

Attitudes after self-defense

The better you know your neighbors, the better they know you — and the more likely they will be to close ranks around you, rather than against you. Those you know less well, or not at all, may not be so inclined.

Social change can happen as a result of your defense of your own life or those of your family. Whenever you use force in self-defense, people will judge you for it. If you've used deadly force resulting in the death of another human being, the people around you will take sides — some of them against you. This is an attempt to isolate the community against the "evil," and can result in emotional trauma to you and your family.

In his excellent books and courses on the use of lethal force, Massad Ayoob talks about the "Mark of Cain Syndrome." The term describes society's very real tendency to shun those who have killed another person, whether or not it's in justifiable self-defense. This tendency is often cited as a major component of Post-Traumatic Stress Disorder (PTSD), and it can have severe psychological and emotional consequences.

I've talked to some people who have killed in legitimate self-defense, and they tell me a lot of people simply stopped talking to them. Even people they thought were friends, people they'd known for some time, avoided them, and their children were no longer allowed to play together. One couple actually had to move to a new community to start their lives over.

I've read about others who have been through similar events. Some reported losing jobs, and others had marriages and relationships break up in the aftermath of a defensive shooting. Even in the best cases, the survivors talked about long-term social isolation and the need for counseling for both themselves and their families.

There is a persistent belief that talking about these post-incident issues makes them into a self-fulfilling prophecy. Some believe ignoring the problem makes it less likely to manifest itself, but I don't agree. Neither do the mental health professionals who deal with these issues on a daily basis. Understanding the emotional and psychological effects of a life-threatening incident is an important first step in Recovery.

Faith as a Recovery tool

Massad Ayoob once told me that he noticed people with strong religious faith seem to recover from these events with less trauma than those who do not have such faith. This might be due to several factors, but I believe one of the most important is the communities to which people of faith belong. Having people around who share your beliefs and also believe in you no doubt contributes greatly to your own resilience. (I'm not saying the atheists in the audience should feign belief just to become a member of such a community, only that it seems to be a great advantage to those who believe. It might be worth seeking out a similar community based on some other kind of shared belief.)

Don't be afraid to seek help

Finally, it's important to seek counseling when you need it. In the past, our society saw admitting to PTSD as "diminishing manhood" or contributing to the decline of morality. Soldiers and police officers who survived brutal encounters were not encouraged to seek help for their emotional issues, and in many cases were punished for doing so. Seeing a psychiatrist was the death knell for promotions and often marked the termination of otherwise successful careers.

While we (thankfully) know better today, those attitudes still surface every so often. A subtle social pressure exists to avoid counseling for

PTSD, and even the term itself is not always accepted. Don't let this deter you from seeking the help you need.

Whether you're recovering from a self-defense incident, a devastating flood, or even a car crash, you may feel after-effects. If you find yourself having flashbacks or nightmares, avoiding reminders of the event, or having negative thoughts or emotions, seek counseling. As part of your Recovery planning, learn about the symptoms and treatment for PTSD *. Take advantage of any help offered. If you know someone who is recovering from a traumatic incident, be a good neighbor and direct them to get the help they need.

The best Deter, Detect, and Respond plans in the world do you no good if your life is sidelined because of the emotional aftershocks. Make psychological Recovery part of your planning.

*www.ptsd.va.gov/public/PTSD-overview/basics/symptoms_of_ptsd.asp

EVERYDAY READY

It's tempting to think of personal safety and preparedness like a wedding: You plan for months, spend lots of money, and then the day comes you dress up in clothes that you'll likely never wear again to participate in an event that (we all hope) only happens once.

Many people look at their preparedness planning the same way: "Gosh, that's a lot of time/effort/money/space to expend on something I'll never use." I'd like to introduce you to a different mindset.

Preparedness needs to be thought of in terms of how it protects you today — this minute. It's not a matter of being ready for the once-in-a-lifetime event, but rather being prepared for anything that might happen **today**.

"If it comes, I'm ready for it"

This is the idea behind the term everyday ready: You're prepared for the plausible things that might happen today, from the mundane to the exceptional. You've taken commonsense precautions and made reasonable plans and preparations to get through whatever life may throw at you.

You're not preparing for some far-off day. You're preparing for what might happen to you right now. Disasters large and small, personal and communal, happen every day all over this planet. Your plans, skills, and gear exist in case that day happens in your neighborhood.

Everyday ready means you've committed to putting together the equipment you need and the training to use it, and having those ready to go at a moment's notice. It doesn't mean sealing yourself up in a bunker. It means taking those skills and tools with you wherever you go (as much as is practical, of course) in case you need them today.

The essence of everyday ready is to have what you need at hand when you need it. That may mean knowledge, skill, or gear, but the concept is the same: to be resilient enough to get past the difficulty you face right now.

Everyday ready is the state where you know you can survive without knowing what you'll need to survive. At the beginning of this book, I talked about the peace that comes from the balance between knowing what you need to do and what you can actually do. Everyday ready is the ultimate expression of that balance.

Anticipation, the planning of Deterrence, Detection, and Response (including Recovery) for each plausible threat, is the key to achieving balance. Equip, Train, and Maintain are how you put those plans into action, but always with an eye to keeping balanced. Let your matrixes show you what you need to do and when. Think not in terms of what's fun, but rather in terms of what will keep you in balance.

Being everyday ready

Achieving everyday readiness requires you to do the work and preparation talked about in the rest of this book. As you reach the stage of being able to deal with more and more events, from the small to the large, you'll find yourself becoming more at ease.

When you can look around wherever you are and know what action you would take if something happened, you're everyday ready. When you know you have the tools to Respond to a range of plausible threats, you're everyday ready. When your skills are sufficient to keep yourself and others alive in the worst likely case, you're everyday ready.

Back to the rainsuit analogy I used at the start of this book: When you know you have something with you that will keep you dry in the storm you see on the horizon, you're not worried about getting under a roof. You're ready for the rain. Every day.

EPILOGUE: WHEN IS IT "ENOUGH"?

Preparedness can become a never-ending spiral. Some people spend so much time preparing, they forget to live their life. Their fear of the future becomes all-consuming and they spend all their discretionary funds and waking hours on their preparedness plans.

How do you know when you've reached the point where you're done? How do you know when to stop?

Balance, revisited

There is a recent lifestyle concept called by many words, but my favorite is "enoughness." That's not a real word, of course, but it's been coined by those in the personal-growth field to denote a state in which you have sufficient resources (of whatever kind) to address your needs, but neither needing nor wishing for excess. The idea of this sufficiency movement is to bring your wants in line with your needs so you're happy when you reach that point of sufficiency, of "enoughness." By reaching that point, adherents feel, you achieve an ideal level of self-satisfaction. You have everything you need, and you don't have to worry about spending your resources frivolously or wastefully.

The whole point of preparedness, of striving for personal security, is so you can live your life in peace. It's hard to be at peace when you're constantly preparing for war. This is why I began this book by talking about achieving peace through the balance of what you *need* to do and what you *can* do. That is the personal-safety version of "enoughness": you've done what you can rationally and realistically do to prevent plausible threats from impacting your life, but with the understanding that nothing you could possibly do would prepare you for **everything**.

As you've learned in this book, you do this by first reaching an understanding of the threats that can disrupt your life, then doing the things that prevent those disruptions from radically altering or ending your life (or the lives of your loved ones). Once those two goals have been met, you've achieved your own "enoughness" — it's time for you to enjoy the life you've gone to the trouble to protect!

Creeping paranoia

Familiarity is a peculiar thing. It enables you to see things others don't, because you know what to look for, but in extreme cases it can lead you to see things that don't exist.

Veteran police officers know this tendency all too well. After some time dealing with the dregs of society — the thieves, rapists, muggers, child molesters, and murderers — they can develop the tendency to see everyone as a bad guy. Every person on the street, even their neighbors, can end up being seen as just another future inmate.

It's not limited to dealing with bad guys, either. I once knew a brilliant fellow who worked as an epidemiologist, and he looked at every disease outbreak as a potential pandemic. When flu season rolled around, he became visibly nervous. I also knew one of his several ex-wives, who told me that, although he was a kind and loving man, he was also impossible to live with because he saw death wherever he looked.

I've known Y2K (remember that?) true believers who spent all their spare time and money stockpiling food, medicine, fuel, and ammunition for the impending collapse of society, and hardcore search-and-rescue personnel who wouldn't step off pavement for a picnic with their family unless they had on their survival backpack.

As Abraham Maslow pointed out, if the only tool you have is a hammer, you're likely to look at every problem as a nail. While this will probably anger hardcore Second Amendment activists, I see this frequently in cases where a person's only self-defense mechanism is a firearm. They do seem to use the firearm when it isn't appropriate or even necessary.

This can affect anyone who is deeply involved in preparedness, whether dealing with self-defense, disaster survival, or even food storage. It's easy to become paranoid when you spend too many of your waking moments preparing for a fight or collapse that (hopefully) never happens. It's easy to lose perspective, to the detriment of your relationships (and perhaps even your health).

Avoiding obsession

I want to emphasize this point, because it's so easy to get bogged down in the fear of preparing or in the consumptive orgy of buying more things because you "need" them: **The reason Adaptive Personal Security exists is so you can live your life**. Never lose sight of that. It's my fervent belief that, by systematically preparing for the plausible dangers you face in your life, you can relieve yourself of the burden that comes from unresolved uncertainty about the future.

At the same time, by striving for balance and not delving into any one area to the point you become obsessed, you avoid the creeping paranoia that afflicts others. When you've reached a point of "enoughness" in any one area or subject, you move on to the next thing (or maybe next several things) and devote your attention there. Your filled Matrixes serve as proof that you've done enough by your own measures.

Sleep soundly knowing you've done what you can, and what you've done is enough. No greater peace exists.

FREE PREPPING FOR LIFE WORKSHEETS

Remember to download your free Worksheet Pack to help you plan your preparedness activities!

These are the same worksheets I use in my preparedness planning. Inside the Worksheet Pack you'll find:

- The Preparedness Inventory worksheet, to help you catalog what you've already done and put it all into proper context to help you move forward
- The Threat Assessment worksheet, to help you figure out what you should really prepare for
- The Adaptive Personal Security Matrix, which is the key to planning and charting all your preparedness activities

All of them are in PDF format so you can print out as many as you need, plus I've included an Excel spreadsheet version of the Threat Assessment worksheet for instant Risk Index calculation!

Get your Worksheet Pack, FREE, at this link:

www.getgrant.us/prepping

FACEBOOK DISCUSSION GROUP

If you have a Facebook account, please join me and the other readers of Prepping For Life in our own private Facebook group!

The Prepping For Life Facebook group is a place for you to discuss all of the important topics in this book. You can ask questions, get answers, network with other preparedness-minded people, and get the motivation you need to stay on the path to balance and peace.

It's a private group, so outsiders can't see what's posted there. Your discussions will only be visible to other like-minded members!

Here's the link to our group page. Just click on "Join" and you'll be added to the group:

www.facebook.com/groups/preppingforlife

ABOUT THE AUTHOR

The world can be a dangerous place. It's always been that way, though. And yet that doesn't seem to make people feel any better. Everyone seems to be scared of what the future might bring, scared because they're not prepared for it.

How much happier and more fulfilling would your life be if you could live a life free from that kind of fear and anxiety? It's possible; you can get there, you can make yourself and your family safer from the dangers you face — no matter what the form.

I want to help by finding the best information from the most reliable sources and distilling it into relevant, actionable lessons that you can put to use in your life. In my books and workshops I focus on teaching the most important skills, and doing so in a way that leads you to competency and long-term retention. Whether self defense, situational awareness, or disaster preparedness, I always focus on you, your life, and your needs.

I've been studying the field of self defense and personal preparedness since the early 1990s. I've attended hundreds of hours of training in many related fields, from defensive firearms to immediate trauma care to how predatory criminals think, all aimed at learning what's valuable and what's not. I even did the coursework for a degree in Emergency Management, just to find out how professionals plan for a wide range of potential hazards!

What I learned from my education is that there's no "one size fits all" solution to personal security, and that glib answers don't keep people safer. I've taken this insight and applied it to everything I teach. The result is the information that I've put into my many books, workshops and classes.

The basics of self sufficiency were a large part of my growing up on a small farm in rural Oregon during the turbulence of the 1960s and 1970s. My Father was, despite his lack of formal education, an intelligent man for whom community service was a way of life. More than once I saw him stand up for people of all colors when he felt they were being poorly treated. From him I learned that everyone matters and that helping people conquer their fears is a noble act.

My childhood was filled with typical rural activities such as hunting and fishing, and guns were a natural part of that ecosystem. On a farm the firearm is a tool, just like any other tool, and they represented work. I learned they have a proper use and a misuse. As a consequence I neither feared nor fetishized them.

I believe in the civil rights of all Americans, including the right to defend oneself using the most efficient means possible. I also believe that with rights always come responsibilities, and that we often talk far too much about the former and not nearly enough about the latter. I remain a strong believer in the value of our country's Constitution — even if our application of that document is sometimes flawed.

My Father's lessons have not been lost on me, and as a result I fight to be the voice of reason, the "adult in the room", to remind people that there is often more than one valid point of view. Today I put everything I've learned to use on my own small farm in the mountains of rural Oregon, where I live with my wife and far too many cats.

www.grantcunningham.com
info@grantcunningham.com

OTHER TITLES BY GRANT CUNNINGHAM

Protect Yourself With Your Snubnose Revolver

Handgun Training - Practice Drills For Defensive Shooting

Defensive Revolver Fundamentals

Defensive Pistol Fundamentals

Gun Digest Book Of The Revolver

Shooter's Guide To Handguns

Prepping for Life:

The Balanced Approach to Personal Security and Family Safety

By Grant Cunningham

Published by Personal Security Institute LLC

Click or visit:

www.grantcunningham.com

Made in the USA
Lexington, KY
24 October 2017